TO: LINDA

THANKS FOR ALL THE
KINDNESSES OVER THE YEARS!
TAKE GREAT CARE OF FEDEX!

DAVID ZANIA

ENGAGING YOUR YOUR TEAM

LESSONS FOR SERVANT LEADERSHIP

DAVID ZANCA

innovo
PUBLISHING

Published by Innovo Publishing, LLC
www.innovopublishing.com
1-888-546-2111

Providing Full-Service Publishing Services for Christian Authors, Artists & Ministries:
Books, eBooks, Audiobooks, Music & Film

ENGAGING YOUR TEAM
Lessons for Servant Leadership

Library of Congress Control Number: 2018938459
ISBN: 978-1-61314-433-6

Cover Design & Interior Layout: Innovo Publishing, LLC

Printed in the United States of America
U.S. Printing History
First Edition: April 2018

CONTENTS

CHAPTER TWO: LEADERSHIP WISDOM

CHAPTER THREE: MANAGERIAL LESSONS

CHAPTER FOUR: CAREER LESSONS

ILLUSTRATIONS

FOREWORD

The first thirty years of my more than five decades in business were heavily influenced by being part of Tom Watson Jr.'s IBM and Wayne Calloway's PepsiCo. Both came to be known as great "leadership academies," turning out thousands of CXOs across hundreds of corporations. In those companies, I came to appreciate that of all the things that matter to long-term success, leadership and culture matter the most. I believe so passionately in the importance of leadership and culture that I founded the Feld Group Institute, where we are building a generation of future CXO-level leaders for the challenges of a rapidly evolving world. And, throughout my career, I have voraciously consumed leadership books and even written a couple myself. When David asked me to look at his book, I was honored.

A couple of things struck me about the content and structure that differentiates this book from the rest. First, the content is totally based on common sense wisdom and not scientific analysis. It might seem odd that I focus on that aspect, but common sense is not that common anymore. With the accelerated pace of business and technology and the fluid nature of careers and companies, many leaders and executives have forgotten that the same "human" things that motivated people for generations are still highly valued. Things like human decency, a kind word, and honest feedback still matter (a lot).

Our Feld Group Institute is based on a framework first shared in my book *Blind Spot*. There are four planks of a compelling strategy agenda (*why, what, how,* and *who*) and a time-boxed plank of *when* (the journey). What David writes about in this book corresponds to the *who* plank of our framework. During our work on the *who* plank with our clients, we stress the human factor and its importance on organizational success. Specifically, we reference four principles: leadership matters, organization structure matters, performance management matters, and culture matters. The context and stories in this book capture the power that a caring, common sense leader, like David, has on an organization's productivity and quality of life, all congruent to those four principles.

I've personally worked around David for almost a decade at FedEx, and he has now captured in words exactly how he managed himself, his projects, his teams, and his peers, regardless of how difficult the situation. He has made tangible in the book what appeared to be intangible.

The second thing I thought very valuable was the structure of the book. It's written almost as a series of short stories that are easy to read but in a structure that flows from story to story. As a result, it can be read cover to cover or be referred to as one standalone story at a time.

There are many dimensions to leadership, and in this book, David speaks from his heart about the dimensions he is most comfortable with—the practical, human side of leadership. And that's great, because as I have already said, it still matters (a lot).

Charlie Feld
Founder, Feld Group Institute,
Author of *Blind Spot: A Leader's Guide to IT-Enabled Business Transformation* and *The Calloway Way: Results & Integrity*

PREFACE

We were in the middle of a grueling deposition, establishing the facts of who, when, and what, when the plaintiff's attorney changed the pace entirely and asked me, "How would you define leadership?" For a split second, my mind raced through the facts of the case, trying to figure out the relevance of the question. But just as quickly, my instinct kicked in, and I calmly replied, "It's motivating a group of people to achieve a common objective."

That may not be the dictionary definition of leadership, but I was pretty happy with my answer. It reflected how I think of myself as a leader: a person who can bring a group together and accomplish a goal. Many people think of leaders as being visionaries or having loud, bold personalities. And I agree; those can be leaders. But as I learned in my career, leadership comes at all levels and in multiple forms.

WHY THIS BOOK?

My form of leadership reflected my personality: tending toward the quiet, humble, and kind end of the spectrum. I was fortunate to have had some success with this "nice guy" style, including the financial ability to retire early in my career. Colleagues, friends, and family seemed to admire my calm, even approach and often reached out for advice on leadership and career-related questions.

In coaching sessions and informal conversations, we would discuss different leadership styles and situations. Having time to reflect before and after these sessions, I realized that my style of leadership had morphed over the course of a thirty-two-year career, and it was the final twelve years where I actively sought to be a humbler servant leader.

In large part, I believe that my teams respected and benefited from this leadership approach. So after more than a little reflection, I decided I should share important lessons I learned by writing this book. In these pages, I also sought to make clear that leadership is a journey.

At the time I write this book, there is another reason why it is important that servant leadership and civility be discussed as a successful method of accomplishing important goals. The United States is witnessing a divisive brand of leadership from both major political parties. Interest groups on both sides push one-sided agenda and spin information to further divide the population. The dialogue is polluted with insults, threats, and harassment. The vitriol has spilled out to a point where suggested violence (a celebrity holding a mock severed head of the President) and actual violence (a targeted shooting of Republican congressmen) flood the news waves. If ever there were a time not to emulate our political leaders and celebrities, this might be the time.

I hope we are not teaching a generation of leaders how to behave based on the political leadership demonstrated in the past fifteen years. Instead, we need our rising leaders to look for role models who understand the need for servant leaders who value others, respect differing opinions, and accept the necessity of compromise.

For the purposes of this book, I want to clarify a distinction in how I perceive leadership: the frontline leadership of leading a team to a common goal versus the executive leadership of setting vision, defining strategy, and steering a course. Both are critical to the success of an organization, and some of the skills and talents needed are similar. However, we have to make sure we have gradations in leadership; not everyone should be defining the vision, and not everyone should be managing the team. My primary focus is on the leader of the team trying to achieve the goal. However, many of the lessons also apply to the executive who is defining vision and strategy.

WHERE DID THE LESSONS COME FROM?

After more than thirty years in the business world, I have had the opportunity to develop leadership skills through observation, study, training, and practice. My responsibilities placed me in senior management roles at FedEx and on the Board of Directors at Interline Brands. In both cases, I worked with outstanding leaders.

Having learned from some of the greatest leaders in the industry, I have also had the privilege of learning from great men in my private life, whether from within the family or at our churches. Sketching together their styles, methods, and manners with their achievements gave me the opportunity to craft my own leadership style.

While I do not believe I am as effective as any of my mentors at any single attribute of leadership, I do believe that the cumulative influence of their styles created an effective leader within me—effective enough that many people have asked for coaching and insight.

In the coming pages are lessons that I learned; in fact, some of the lessons come the hard way—from mistakes that I made. This is one way I can share my experiences with others. The lessons are categorized to help clarify the purpose and intent of each. Therefore, it is important to define the categories:

Servant Leadership: These lessons come from learnings along my journey where the servant leader thinks of others first, acts with humility, and maintains a broad perspective on purpose, mission, and values. I learned that demeanor and style could have a major impact on workforce morale, culture, and productivity.

Leadership: Through opportunities to serve with numerous outstanding leaders, I observed how they responded to differing situations by making wise decisions and connecting with their constituency. This collection of lessons focuses on the actions and processes a leader can take to make good decisions and maintain an engaged organization.

Managerial: Peter Drucker famously said that "Management is doing things right." These lessons focus on tips to make both the frontline and senior level manager effective.

Career: As we progress in our lives and careers, it is always helpful when someone shares their learnings. These lessons concentrate on career path and choices you may face as you progress.

INFLUENCES ON MY LEADERSHIP PERSPECTIVES

Many times you find references to military leadership principles and quotations from generals such as Eisenhower, Patton, Schwarzkopf, and Powell. There are a number of reasons for this.

First, the military has developed and codified leadership practices for thousands of years. The consequences of leadership in the military are certainly direr than those in most business situations. Life and death decisions hinge on training, discipline, and leadership. Extending those practices to other professions provides a great framework for anyone truly interested in leading under challenging situations. Second, my immediate family served in the military, and I have great respect for the role of leadership in the service of our country. My father was career US Army; my oldest brother was career US Air Force; my next brother was a career US Army officer who was killed in action, serving as a platoon leader. Third, I have benefited from the application of many of those military leadership principles in the business world. At FedEx Express, *The Manager's Guide* defines expectations of each manager in the company. The opening chapters on leadership attributes and styles are directly influenced by founder, Fred Smith's, Marine Corp training.

The US Marine Corp was commissioned in 1775, nearly a year before the Declaration of Independence, to serve and protect a newly formed naval fleet. Their leadership training and teamwork are perhaps unparalleled. In the *Marine Corp Manual*, it defines core values, leadership traits, and leadership principles expected of a marine. These are almost completely applicable to the business world. Fred Smith was a marine officer who served two tours of duty in Vietnam. As he built FedEx, he translated the marine leadership traits and principles into what would work in Corporate America.

From the *Marine Corp Manual*:

> **Core Values**: *Honor, Courage, and Commitment*
>
> **Leadership Traits**: *Integrity, Knowledge, Courage, Decisiveness, Initiative, Tact, Judgment, Justice, Enthusiasm, Bearing, Endurance, Unselfishness, and Loyalty*
>
> **Principles:**
>
> - *Be technically and tactically proficient*
>
> - *Know yourself and seek self-improvement*
>
> - *Know your Marines and look out for their wealth*

- *Keep your Marines informed*

- *Set the example*

- *Ensure the task is understood, supervised, and accomplished*

- *Train your Marines as a team*

- *Make sound and timely decisions*

- *Develop a sense of responsibility among your subordinates*

- *Employ your unit in accordance with its capabilities*

- *Seek responsibility and take responsibility for your actions*

From these values and principles, the FedEx culture was born.

Another major influence upon me has been my wife and her family. Ginny is a natural-born leader. Whatever the job, role, or task, she can see the big picture, create a vision, and then motivate a group to achieve that vision. As a result, Ginny can be described by the phrase, "The world beats a path to her door." Local and national charitable and social organizations as well as foundations have asked her to serve as chairman or to join their board or executive committees. Furthermore, the example set by Ginny's parents, grandparents, aunts, and uncles deeply affected me. They were highly respected businessmen and women, devoted to their family and also dedicated church leaders. They treated everyone with respect. They were the model of civility and politeness. And they had great senses of humor! My admiration of Ginny's family was so great that I told my own mother I really admired them because they were the "all-American family." My mother looked at me disdainfully and asked, "We are *not* the 'all-American family'?"

Clearly, I had stepped into a mess. "Well, no," I tried to explain. We did not have a minister, a Boy Scout council executive, an Eagle Scout, the founders of a church, the founder of a kindergarten, the lay leader of a church, a leader in the community, and three generations of family living within twenty miles of one another. I would have been better served saying they were the prototypical "Norman Rockwell family" because our family was very "all-American."

My parents were gold star parents. My father was career army, two of my brothers were career military, and my other two brothers were like me—college educated and productive citizens. It was wrong of me to tell my gold star parent someone else's family was more all-American than theirs. My family had a service commitment with respect to the military and the nation. What we did not have was the extended family and the service mentality that Ginny's family projected into the community, the church, and the neighborhood. My parents were great people, but in my childhood, they did not take visible leadership roles beyond coaching little league baseball. Ginny's family was the opposite: They served in the military as required, but not as a vocation. They served the church, the community, and others as a vocation. I could learn a lot from them regarding servant leadership.

You will also find a number of references to the Bible and of our family commitment to the Christian church. If religion in general or Jesus as your Savior is not your "thing," please don't be offended. One thing we should be able to agree with is that the Bible, with the wisdom of Proverbs, rich stories such as the loyalty of Ruth, the courage of Deborah and Esther, the triumphs and flaws of King David, and the poetry of Psalms, is great literature from which we can learn. The Old Testament features numerous examples of leaders, such as Moses and Nehemiah, dealing with difficult situations. The New Testament features a set of leaders, namely Jesus and Paul, who face a different proposition. Whether you believe in the resurrection or not, Jesus was a real historical figure—a wise teacher and a leader—and we can learn from His example.

Over the years, I have found most people whom I consider role models are persons of faith. These men and women are true servant leaders who behave within a framework of values passed down through their faiths. Most of these role models, because of my limited exposure, have been leaders influenced by Judeo-Christian values. As my universe has expanded, I have come to admire a number of Muslim and Hindu leaders. The common thread between these role models is not a singular faith but is instead a core foundation of faith, commitment to values, tolerance, and disposition to serve others.

HOW TO USE THIS BOOK

As you read through the lessons in this book, remember that these come from my personal perspectives, a thirty-two-year career starting as a programmer and working up to executive-level management, and a seat on a board of a publicly traded company. Therefore, the lessons range across the spectrum of categories mentioned above, and every lesson may not apply to the situation in which each reader finds himself or herself. Many of these you will recognize or think are common sense. The truth of the matter is that most people know many of these practices, but few actually follow them. Hopefully, you will see the applicability to you, your boss, or the next stage in your career, and you will use them.

You might use this as a tool where each week you read a new lesson and work to incorporate it within your life. Most likely you are already practicing many of these lessons, so you might read and skip over to another lesson. Hopefully, each week you will find a new, applicable lesson out of the sixty lessons in the book.

Another approach to using this book is to read the chapters corresponding to where you are in your career. Use the lessons to address specific situations you are facing in your current role. Suggested areas of focus are as follows:

For All Readers

Key behaviors a servant leader exhibits are highlighted in chapter one. Regardless of where you find yourself in life or career, chapter one should apply to all. This is especially true in a world where civility, compromise, respect, and service are values that many of our leaders are not demonstrating. Chapter four will be of interest to all readers as well. Being at your best will make you a better leader.

Middle or Senior Management

Chapter two primarily focuses on lessons for someone who is in a decision-making role, leading multiple groups.

Frontline or Middle Management

For the reader in frontline or middle management, chapter three, Managerial Lessons, focuses on many tips useful in his or her daily role. Many of these lessons offer best practices for managing or motivating your team.

Early in a Career

If you are early in your career, chapter four, Career Lessons, will be particularly interesting. These lessons focus on career movement and planning.

Business Schools/MBA Programs/College Students

For business schools, MBA programs, and business-minded students, this book can serve as a supplemental text to a broader curriculum on leadership. The servant leadership framework, independent lessons, and takeaway discussion topics lend themselves well to classroom, online, and group discussions forums.

A final suggested method to using this book is to do an honest self-assessment of your strengths and weaknesses and then target lessons addressing how you can continuously improve areas of strength or improve areas of weakness. For example, you might assess your abilities according to the following and choose your area of focus:

Strengths/Weaknesses					
Service: aptitude to serve others and make sacrifices	5	4	3	2	1
Risk: recognition of and willingness to accept risk	5	4	3	2	1
Values: ability to articulate and demonstrate	5	4	3	2	1
Managerial: practices to best achieve results	5	4	3	2	1
Leadership: skills to motivate and care for a team	5	4	3	2	1
Lifestyle: personal, spiritual, and physical health	5	4	3	2	1
Career: satisfaction and proactive plans to manage your career	5	4	3	2	1

At the end of each lesson is a takeaway and action item to help you put the lesson into practice. Think about the questions posed, and jot down thoughts on how you can apply the lesson.

Supplemental to this book are additional lessons published on my website, *SpainwoodConsulting.com*. The website also includes a number of videos sharing perspectives on selected topics in this book.

Should you find the content useful and desire to share with your team or organization, please contact my firm, Spainwood Consulting, for information regarding bulk book order discounts, speaking engagements, and seminar sessions. Additionally, short-term coaching engagements are available for individuals.

FINAL THOUGHTS

To re-enforce the importance of serving and supporting others, any profits generated from the sale of this book will be contributed to charitable organizations that are building future generations of leaders. These organizations teach the importance of values and offer leadership opportunities for the participants.

As you will discover in this book, my career concentrated on information technology exclusively and its strategic importance. Technology is evolving faster than ever, and the impact is massive. Companies such as Apple, Amazon, and Uber are redefining entire industries with web-service-based strategies that disintermediate providers from their customers. Consumers instantly have decision-making information at their fingertips. With the ubiquity of cell phone cameras, privacy has been challenged. Hackers and scammers threaten every institution and individual.

The lessons within this book do not pertain to information technology but to leadership practices in general. For readers with interest in more specific best practices in information technology, please visit *SpainwoodConsulting.com*. Lessons related specifically to information technology management are shared there.

In this book, you will find a few illustrations. My learning style is visual. I would doodle on conference calls, generating large-scale doodles. In meetings, I would sketch process flows, diagram the problem, or even create a design of a solution. When faced with an absurd situation at work that would be comical if reasonable thinking did not intercede, I would make a note and later sketch a satirical cartoon. I have included a few of the doodles and cartoons that might pertain to a lesson here and there. Some of these cartoons came from my consulting days, some from corporate life, and others from stories shared with me by friends at different companies. You will also find more illustrations and cartoons at *SpainwoodConsulting.com*. Hopefully, they will result in someone's enjoyment. Most likely, mine.

Figure 1: Corporate Art of David Zanca

(Visit *SpainwoodConsulting.com* to see more illustrations.)

CHAPTER ONE:
SERVANT LEADERSHIP JOURNEY

ONE: INTRODUCTION

Allow me to begin with a confession: I made a lot of mistakes in my career. And in the beginning, I was not a servant leader. I was around servant leaders in my personal life and at church, but I did not grasp the concept until after I went to work at FedEx. By the end of my journey, I was a much better manager and leader than I was early in my career. This chapter shares lessons and practices of a servant leader, but I have to say that someone who worked with me in those early years might not recognize these as my traits. Some people are true natural-born leaders, and within those are subsets that are natural-born servant leaders. For example, people who always knew they were called to service in the ministry, health care, or public safety may inherently possess the attributes of a servant leader. Fortunately, for the rest of us, we grow and mature, listen and observe, and have an opportunity to become servants.

I began my professional career in the consulting division of Arthur Andersen & Co. At that point in time, Andersen was one of the "Big Eight" accounting firms. Andersen was known for its strong culture, high integrity, and progressive consulting practice, which concentrated on information technology services. The culture was a performance-based culture that was deemed "up or out." In other words, you were succeeding and on track to progress to the next level, or you were counseled out of the firm. There was no tolerance for people who plateaued in their career.

When I began my career with FedEx, I had nearly eleven years of performance-based culture programmed into me. FedEx was another company with a very strong culture, but it was based on a servant leader model where the role of the manager was to knock down barriers, clear paths, secure what their team needed to be successful, and get out of the way so team members could deliver. The emphasis was on making teams successful because the very nature of the business required that teams and organizations work together to make the FedEx network work. Customers' packages had to be picked up on time, moved to an airport ramp by an exact time, loaded, flown to the hub (primarily in Memphis), sorted in a very short time period, and then reloaded onto a plane. After being flown to the destination city, they had to be unloaded and moved to a local station for final sorting onto delivery vans, which had to begin deliveries on a very specific schedule. Meanwhile, package information and tracking information had to be made available to customers and other departments. This model required everyone to work in synchronicity to accomplish the daily business cycle. And, by the way, this is the simplest side of the business, as there are many other dimensions that complicate this ballet even more.

Needless to say, this is a completely different environment from the consulting world, where each client and project is independent from another. The FedEx focus on the success of the team rather than the individual was indicative of this difference. I loved the change in the beginning and took pride in caring for my team members—their success, their development, their families, and their livelihood.

In hindsight, I can now see that shortly thereafter, I was backsliding into the individualistic performance-based model of my past. I am not proud to say it, but when in charge of a high pressure, high visibility project—which also involved my former firm, Andersen—I settled back in to their leadership model. I valued people who would deliver, regardless of the wake they might leave behind. We expected long hours and weekends of work like the consultants were accustomed to working. In effect, we were trying to work within their culture, not ours.

However, while working with a group of teams to accomplish a major part of the program, I witnessed the interdependence of the teams, the necessity to cooperate, and the personal care and respect everyone had for one another. This made it clear that the power of organization radiated not from the individual but from the collective. The manager and/or leader was important, but the passion and commitment of the teams was the critical factor. My style began to revert back to the FedEx way. I found myself in a role where I was directly in touch with both the senior leadership team and the frontline employee. Suddenly, I felt an obligation to each—to the senior team, to make sure their strategies were being communicated and executed, and to the team members, to make sure they understood why we were doing things and that senior management heard their concerns.

At our church, our new senior minister introduced us to Henry Nouwen's book *In the Name of Jesus*. Nouwen, a noted theologian and author, wrote this book after leaving his position at Harvard University to spend ten years living with and serving handicapped and disabled people in Toronto. For the purposes of our new minister, he wanted us to understand that ministry was a call to servant leadership where everyone humbly served the other, including the least amongst us. In the process of studying and reading commentaries about the book, the applicability of the concepts to leadership in a secular world struck me.

Clearly, the point of serving others at work was relevant. More powerful, however, were Nouwen's points that a true servant leader does not seek recognition and glory but rather, through their work with others, allows them to shine. The servant leader serves in the background and, to most, is irrelevant. They fight the tendency to be a "star," with the implications that the "star" can accomplish things on their own, because in most situations, they cannot. Additionally, Nouwen makes the point that leaders seeking power typically do so for a lack of intimacy and inability to relate with their followers. What occurs is a power-control model that is authoritarian in style, treating others with little respect.

Given what I was experiencing at church and at work, Nouwen's points resonated with me. It also fit my introverted personality type. Being a leader did not mean you had to be a "star," loud, or flashy. It meant helping your team be successful, letting them take the credit, and not being seduced by the temptation of power. This guided a lot of career choices I made. I would seek a few positions where there was opportunity to make a difference, but not for purposes of building a power base. Organizationally, I would give up groups if we believed it was in the best interest of the company; though I will say, most of my colleagues on the receiving end viewed it as a power play—an "I win, you lose" proposition. Truly, I wanted others to succeed, receive recognition, and have opportunities, even to the point of retiring early so another generation of leadership could have their day. This was the legacy that a teaching such as Nouwen's had upon me.

In my case, the recipe to develop into a servant leader was complex:

1. Start with a family devoted to serving in the military;

2. Add two counterculture work experiences;

3. Mix in strong church influence and outstanding family role models;

4. Blend in exposure to outstanding teams and passionate team members;

5. Experience a short C-level role;

6. Add a pinch of the leadership training I was receiving through the FedEx Leadership Institute;

7. Stir in the FedEx *Manager's Guide*; and

8. Top it with working alongside some great servant leaders.

Then bake slowly and serve. Refresh with training classes such as Team Trek, Human Performance Institute, or culture training.

Because I was not a natural-born servant leader, I still revert to other styles. That is why I made the following list of servant leadership lessons; this reminds me of what is important. If I can keep the core tenets of treating people with respect, putting others first, and serving with a glad heart in my approach, the results will be good.

LESSON 1

SERVE OTHERS FIRST

Officers eat last. (US Marine Corp)

T his is the basic tenet of servant leadership. The leader puts others first, and in doing so, demonstrates respect and love. It shows that leadership is not about power and authority. Leadership is about making sure others are empowered and cared for.

EXAMPLE

In the realm of spiritual leaders, there are many great examples, such as Mother Teresa, who served others and, through her service, set an example to follow. Her service was not to the rich or privileged but to the sick and impoverished. The theologian and author Henri Nouwen served handicapped and mentally disabled persons in Toronto for ten years. Through the process, he discovered that service to those who cannot help themselves was a spiritual gift—to both the recipient and the giver. He noted that through service, one gives and receives love, and one learns and grows personally while benefiting others.

EXAMPLE

The New Testament provides the example of the ultimate servant leader, Jesus, washing the feet of His disciples. This gesture provides a symbol of the leader not just serving His team but lowering Himself to perform one of the most unpleasant tasks of that day: washing a person's filthy feet. In the book of John, Jesus demonstrates that no task is beneath a leader, and the act of service is one of sacrifice, care, love, and respect for the recipient. He sets the example, which He instructs His disciples to follow.

EXAMPLE

A much different example of servant leadership comes from a totally different source: the US Marines Corp. The marines live the example every day with their practice of "Officers Eat Last." This has been generalized by authors such as Simon Sinek as "Leaders Eat Last" to apply the concept to other disciplines such as businesses, government, and non-profit organizations.[1]

As a leader, it is important to demonstrate this principle on a consistent basis. We would annually hold a barbecue for our hundreds of team members, and the senior team would be cooking and serving. That's one little symbolic gesture, but it can lead to others. When the team is putting in a long night, we would bring in the food and serve them in the workspace, making sure that the "leader eats last." Often, I would give up my seat on a flight for a team member and/or their family.

But in the workplace, the way a servant leader can make the biggest difference is in helping the team be successful by clearing barriers for them, resolving issues in a timely fashion, and supporting them however they need. A manager functioning as a leader serves his or her team in a humble manner. That may include symbolic gestures similar to feet washing, such as doing unpleasant tasks that others might think beneath a leader. For example, we would encourage our management, me included, to cover certain briefings and meetings so team members could concentrate on the most important activities. When the subject was so technical or specific that we needed the team to participate, they would certainly attend. But, we would offload as much as possible from them, demonstrating our servant leadership values.

Takeaway: A servant leader puts the good of the whole ahead of their self-interests. By serving others, they set the example and create an environment of mutual commitment.

- In your role, when do you have opportunities to serve?
- Are there servant leader role models in your organization?
- What do they do that you might emulate?

LESSON 2

STAND UP FOR RIGHT AND FOR GOOD PEOPLE

Find out just what any people quietly submit to and you have the exact measure of the injustice and wrong which will be imposed on them. (Frederick Douglas)

Integrity is often defined as doing the right thing when no one is looking. But, it is also standing up for right when in the face of opposition. There are times when you know something cannot be achieved in a certain time frame, and you have to stand up for your team. You have to make sure they are set up to succeed, not fail. There will be times when people jump to conclusions and incorrectly correlate data points. You have to stand up and use facts to dispute the conclusions. There are times that good people are misunderstood, undervalued, or discriminated against. You have to stand up for those people and be their advocate. Having the personal conviction to do this is hard, but it is the truest test of one's character.

One important aspect to master is discerning when waging a fight in a public setting, such a meeting, is productive, versus publicly lodging a concern and taking the discussion off-line. Sometimes arguing with the boss in front of others works, but other times it is not a productive strategy. You may win, but the boss loses. Follow your gut in those situations, and if you need to take it off-line to avoid embarrassing the boss, make a subtle request to discuss it later. If the situation is one in which there is a disagreement with peers or partners, proceed in public to correct the injustice; if approaching a stalemate, suggest continuing the discussion off-line.

EXAMPLE

As a manager in a project delivery role, one mantra that I lived by was setting the team up for success. We needed to push the team and get the most out of them, so my goal was not to "low ball" or "sandbag," but at the same time, to make sure they were not set with unrealistic expectations that they could not achieve. Once, I went toe to toe with my boss in front of one of his peers on a particular milestone. Eventually, I won the day when this peer weighed in with the perspective that they needed to listen to the person who had done this type of project before. But my relationship with the boss was strained. Maybe I should have tried to table that conversation and go off-line with the boss. In other situations with business partners, I spoke truth as to what was right and achievable, and while they didn't like the answer, they respected the honesty.

EXAMPLE

One of the greatest examples of standing up for right in the workplace was not of my doing—I was a witness. One of my team members stood up in front of the executive leadership and their peers to challenge a specific plan that was flawed. This vice president was passionate in her plea to revisit the plan, arguing that while the intent was good and she did not disagree with the objective, it was wrong in its approach and had serious negative consequences. In this case, good people were going to have their careers, livelihoods, retirements, and self-esteem irreparably impacted. A few peers chirped in but not with the same passion and courage of this woman. I cannot recall what I may have said, but I know I was not vocal and demonstrative in the meeting. Maybe if I had offered my resignation, that could have stopped the train. Maybe others would have followed and joined me. But, I did not.

The vice president who stood up for right was not directly punished or admonished for her actions. As her boss, I would make sure she was not officially reprimanded. But she paid an unofficial price for her stance. She could not let go of the decision to proceed and the consequences that followed. This would haunt her, and she would revisit it as a warning to not let history repeat itself. Unfortunately, that was viewed as bitterness, negativism, and "I told you so." This attitude going forward, not the challenge she made that day, affected her standing with senior, executive, and peer leaders. Regardless, I admired her courage, wished I had more, and resolved not to be silent again. Through her courage and my mistake, I learned a very, very valuable lesson.

Subsequently, when a group of my peers were maligning a very important part of our team and recommending we eliminate an entire workforce location, I relived that prior day. This time, I stood up for what was right and for good people. My peers and I certainly saw attributes, characteristics, contributions, and capabilities of this workforce differently. I stood up for the group and the specific person under attack, as both were good, loyal, productive members of our team. They had a valuable role in our future. Using a few facts, I could rebuke some of the more tangible arguments, turning the debate into a subjective set of arguments. Fortunately, subjectivity did not win.

Takeaway: As Martin Luther King, Jr. said, "Injustice anywhere is a threat to justice everywhere."

- When you see injustice in any form, what do you do? Speak up? Encourage others to act?

- Where are you likely to encounter injustice, and what actions would you take?

- Sometimes standing up for what is right requires a cost. Are you prepared to pay this price? Set your resolve and willingness to pay such a cost before you need to act. Otherwise you may find yourself silent, with an opportunity missed.

LESSON 3

TREAT EVERYONE WITH RESPECT

Afford each person the same respect, support, and fair treatment you would expect if your roles were reversed. Deal with people individually, not as objects who are part of a herd—that's the critical factor. (Coach Bill Walsh)

We have all heard the Golden Rule: *Do unto others as you would have them do unto you.* One important aspect of that rule worth amplifying is treating everyone with respect and courtesy regardless of their role or position. A leader should engage with the team at all levels and respect each individual for their contribution regardless of the perceived importance of the role. This makes everyone feel valuable and like a critical part of the team.

Realize that you are being observed outside of the work environment as well. Your team sees you at the grocery, the airport, the park, in restaurants, and at church. How you treat people in your personal life is noticed. Whether the bagger at the grocery, the counter worker at the airport, a volunteer at church, or someone else, treat everyone, regardless of their role, with dignity and kindness.

EXAMPLE

Within our organizations, we have the "water carriers," the "go-to people," and the "superstars" that do a lot of the heavy lifting and delivery. But for them and for you to succeed, there is a supporting cast that rarely gets noticed. These are the people doing the less exotic tasks: the clerical work, the administrative work, the dirty work, and the daily detailed work. They are administrative assistants, system administrators, entry-level staff, supply clerks, security staff, cafeteria workers, and the cleaning crew. Without them, the "superstars" cannot shine. Each one of them is critical to the success of the organization (if their role isn't critical, it shouldn't exist), and the people working those roles are due your respect and courtesy. Engage with them, get to know them, thank them for what they do, and when given an opportunity, acknowledge them in public. That sets the tone for all that everyone is valuable.

I could always tell the nature of someone with whom I would be working by the way they interacted with my administrative assistant. A visitor who took the time to chat, get to know the people in my office, and build a rapport would be an individual who understood the power of relationships. People who treated the administrative staff poorly—and there were plenty—showed their true nature. They were too important to invest energy with someone they perceived as unimportant to their goals. They underestimated the important role the assistants play. They also misunderstood my opinions on respect and civility.

Takeaway: Treating everyone with respect is always important, but in this contentious world, it is even more critical.

- Is this something you hold as a core value and practice every day?
- What action can you take to ensure you treat everyone with respect?

LESSON 4

TO WHOM MUCH IS GIVEN

From everyone to whom much has been given, much will be required; and from the one to whom much has been entrusted, even more will be demanded. (Luke 12:48)

The true context of this scripture speaks to the followers of Christ who have been given a great amount in a spiritual manner. The scripture is so elegant that when applied to a more material set of blessings, it offers a great lesson for leading our lives and leading one another. So many of us have been blessed with the opportunity of education and employment. Working with a steady income, in a safe environment, and with benefits—though never as generous or plush as one might like—is a real blessing. The vast majority of the world does not enjoy the same blessings. Thus we have been given a great amount, and the scripture tells us that much will be required.

The scripture also speaks to those entrusted with responsibilities such as leadership, stewardship, and management. Of those, "even more will be demanded." The standard for those in positions of authority is and should be greater.

EXAMPLE

This is perhaps my favorite piece of scripture. It resonated with me during the baccalaureate service at my college graduation;

certainly, everyone graduating that day had been blessed with much, and the charge was to do something of meaning with the blessings. As I progressed in my career to the point of being entrusted with the welfare and livelihood of the people in my organization, not to mention the satisfaction of customers' needs and shareholders' expectations, I realized the second half of the scripture applied to me. "Even more" meant I was to be held to a higher standard. I tried to manage and lead to a high set of self-imposed standards, which honestly turned into what I call self-righteousness disorder (SRD). My intent was noble: to meet the charge called out at that baccalaureate service. But I let it go a bit too far and became self-righteous in the process. Thankfully, my family calls me out and reels me in when I get too self-righteous.

This lesson is one that I have tried to share with my children. We are very fortunate with our blessings of a stable and loving family, a nice home, food on the table, and great educational opportunities. As a result, there are great expectations that flow through to them: be good, kind people who, among many responsibilities, seek justice for others. When we can pass along opportunities to the next generation, it's vital that they accept those opportunities, understanding the responsibilities that come with them.

Takeaway: People who recognize they have been given many blessings understand the importance to share their talents through service.

- What gifts or blessings have you received?
- How have you used those to the betterment of others?
- Are you one "to whom much has been entrusted"? If so, what can you do to share your riches?

LESSON 5

WHEN YOU MAKE A MISTAKE, OWN UP

When you make a mistake, own it; when you have a success, share the credit.
(David Zanca)

Invariably, we all make a mistake or two or three in our careers. Sometimes a number gets transposed, a deadline is accidentally missed, something breaks, and so on. It happens. What is important is how you respond when it does happen. My suggestion is to be transparent and honest as to the root cause and how you plan to avoid making the same mistake again. In other words, if you or your team makes a mistake, own it. As noted by authors Doug Guthrie and Sudhir Venkatesh in their article "Creative Leadership: Humility and Being Wrong," "humility and the ability to admit error may be two of the most important qualities a truly creative leader must have."[2]

EXAMPLE

Once, our team missed a major deadline that delayed a number of initiatives for the corporation by roughly two months. As if the delay wasn't bad enough, the effect of the delay rippled into the next wave of projects that were scheduled for later in the year. So the cumulative effect was two or more months of postponement for most projects that year. In this instance, we had followed the processes we normally used, and in previous cases, we would make the deadline with just a little time to spare. However, in this case, we ran out of time. We had checkpoints along the path, and I knew we were cutting this close. But rather than heeding the old line that "past performance is not indicative of future results," I believed we would do what we always did and make the deadline. As we approached the launch hour, we were waiting on the results of a final test run. But the clock moved quicker than the test, and we just ran out of time. Not knowing the final results, we had to delay the launch, and that meant waiting two months for the next opportunity.

As I contemplated this failure, my concerns were twofold: first, the impact to the corporation and the plans for the year; second, for our team who had worked so hard and believed with all their hearts that they were ready to launch. In my eyes, I was responsible to both the corporation and to my team for this failure. I could have pulled contingency levers earlier, which would have resulted in a decoupling of projects and thus allowed for a subset of projects to go forward. So I owned this failure. It was on me for cutting it so close, not choosing to use our contingencies.

The pattern was similar to all the prior patterns, and I thought we'd make it. Certainly, there were contributing factors to why we were running so close to the edge, and those could be identified and remediated for future efforts, but those were not the final cause of the problem. It was a judgment call I made. If someone had to be blamed, it was me. I documented this and published it in an email to a massive distribution list. The note was forwarded all over the corporation when people asked what happened or why projects were delayed.

The feedback to my mea culpa was positive. People appreciated someone taking responsibility and not trying to cover up a problem with a slew of excuses. Our team appreciated that they were not singled out for blame. They did what they could, believed in what they did, and when those test results came in, were proven right that they were ready.

EXAMPLE

In the spring of 2017, United Airlines suffered a public relations disaster when a seated passenger was forcefully removed from a flight in order to make space for a United crewmember. A video of the incident captured an airport security agent pulling the passenger out of his seat and then dragging the passenger down the aisle. The passenger suffered a broken nose, a concussion, and loss of teeth. United's CEO, Oscar Munoz, compounded the mistake by not admitting his team mishandled the situation. He did not apologize right away and instead placed blame elsewhere: on the passenger and the airport security team.

The backlash was unmerciful. United's CEO had to spend weeks backtracking and making amends for the incident. Eventually, he took responsibility for United's systematic failure of policies, procedures, and technology. He admitted United employees were not empowered to do what was right and airline policy was short-sighted, and then he promised major changes would take place to make sure this never happened again on a United flight. He even went further with additional passenger-friendly policy changes to try to build back credibility that United could once again be considered "the Friendly Skies." He did not 'own up' soon enough.

Takeaway: Being accountable for our actions and those of our team is a hallmark of strong leaders.

- When mistakes are made, do you take responsibility or look for someone to blame?
- How can you serve your team by accepting responsibility when a mistake occurs?

LESSON 6

DO THE DIRTY WORK WHEN NECESSARY

Never feel too important to do what needs to be done. (David Zanca)

T his is one of the most important lessons for a servant leader to apply. You are never too important to do the dirty work. Of course, the greatest example comes from the book of Matthew where Jesus sets the example by washing the filthy feet of His disciples. That is dirty work. The servant leader looks for the opportunities to step in and do the unglamorous, mundane, and sometimes dirty work. Doing so clearly demonstrates that you do not consider yourself better than the team. It demonstrates a respect for their time. And it demonstrates a commitment on your part.

This is not to suggest that as a manager, leader, or executive that your time should be completely consumed with setup and breakdown, cleaning up, making the coffee, sorting the mail, etc. But, when necessary and available, being willing to pitch in and help makes a statement to your team. No one is above picking up a piece of trash; no one is too good to make the next pot of coffee; no one is too important to speak to others. So pick up and throw away trash as you leave a meeting. Open and hold doors for people.

Make the next pot of coffee. Be on call in the middle of the night. Little things speak volumes. Don't ask your team to do anything you wouldn't do.

EXAMPLE

Sometimes not everything goes right, or a customer does not like a change you make. In this case, we had made major changes to our website and were actively monitoring social media, web master messages, and calls to our support line. If a customer was irate or just could not figure out the changes, one of our team members would call and talk them through it. However, we received one message to the web master that was rather dark and almost disturbing. In a long, well-written email, the customer berated us for our changes, at one point saying, "someone should shoot the drunken monkey who designed the site and the idiot moron who approved it." The team was upset and brought it to me. As I read the note, I thought, how well written and articulate. Then I got to the "drunken monkey and idiot moron" comment and laughed aloud. Well-written, articulate, and funny. I volunteered to call this customer, much to the relief of our team.

I researched the customer, gained an understanding of their business, and then called. When I reached the owner who had written the email, he was stunned that someone would call, especially a senior officer. Sensing his anxiety, I broke the ice by saying, "My business partner was the drunken monkey that designed the site, and I was the idiot moron who approved it." After that, we had a lovely conversation. He agreed he was a bit harsh in his assessment, and I assured him that we understood that change was painful and no offense was taken. When I relived the call with our team, they were so happy to have that behind them!

EXAMPLE

The times I felt I really needed to do the dirty work was when there was bad news or the situation put one of my managers in a bind. For example, we had a situation where we had to terminate an employee. It could be a contentious situation, and the manager of the employee was about eight months pregnant. She was apprehensive about the process, so this was a time to step in and do what was necessary. In another situation, we had decided we needed to close a location, and nearly fifty people in my organization would lose their jobs. I could delegate this to the vice president of the organization impacted but felt that the right thing was to face the group myself and explain the decision.

In those acts of stepping in, I learned a lot about servant leadership. This was a small flavor of the learnings Henry Nouwen wrote of in his book *In the Name of Jesus*. The process of preparation, performance, and counseling for the affected gave me perspective and growth.

Takeaway: No one is too important or too busy to offer a hand. In doing so, you are setting an example of servitude.

- When can you step in and give a hand?
- Are there other leaders you observe who serve in this fashion?
- How will you institutionalize this behavior so it becomes second nature?

LESSON 7

DEFINE VALUES FOR YOURSELF AND YOUR TEAM

The quality of a leader is reflected in the standards they set for themselves.
(Ray Kroc)

People need to know what their leaders believe in and represent. It provides a meaningful framework for them to fashion their behavior in the completion of their tasks. If leaders do not value teamwork, individuals are empowered to go *rogue*. If leaders do not value open discussion and input, people will be silent and possibly subversive. If leaders do not stress the importance of quality, corners get cut. If leaders do not make it clear that discrimination and harassment are unacceptable, some people become disenfranchised or abused. Leaders need to make it clear to their teams and organizations what they expect and value.

EXAMPLE

Many of the great institutions of learning and leadership in our country are very clear as to the expectations for and values of their students. The military academies not only mold leaders for the armed services, they provide one of the most rigorous educations. The academies all have an honor code that clearly defines the values of honesty, integrity, respect, and civility. This is true at many universities, colleges, and high schools in the nation. The honor code sets clear expectations to students.

EXAMPLE

In Corporate America, corporations create value statements defining their values. At many companies, executives and their board members live by their values, which in turn ripple through the organizations, and, as a result, they are very well esteemed companies. At other corporations, executives may just give lip service to their values or even set values that do not promote teamwork. For example, the CEO of Uber Technologies, Travis Kalanick, defined corporate values which, when combined with his personality, created a toxic environment. The Uber corporate values included values such as "principled confrontation" and "toe-stepping." The board of directors engaged a consultant, former US Attorney General Eric Holder, who recommended they rework their values to promote teamwork and integrity. The board also asked Kalanick to take a leave of absence.[3] Subsequently, over twenty members of management were fired for harassment, and Kalanick resigned.

On the other end of the spectrum is FedEx Corporation. FedEx defined a strong set of values and absolutely lived by them:[4]

People: We value our people and promote diversity in our workplace and in our thinking.

Service: Our absolutely positive spirit puts our customers at the heart of everything we do.

Innovation: We invent and inspire the services and technologies that improve the way we work and live.

Integrity: We manage our operations, finances, and services with honesty, efficiency, and reliability.

Responsibility: We champion safe and healthy environments for the communities in which we live and work.

Loyalty: We earn the respect and confidence of our FedEx people, customers, and investors every day, in everything we do.

Given these examples of corporate values, it becomes incumbent on each leader in an organization to decide what they value and how that fits into larger organizational values. They then have to share those values with their team and live the values. As a leader within FedEx, I personalized the values to my organization and our mission, carefully making sure we stayed true to the corporate values. I called them the A, E, I, O, and US:

A, E, I, O, and US

A - *accountability for your actions: the buck stops here;*

E - *execution with emphasis on quality measurement and reliability;*

I - *integrity in all we do;*

O - *opportunity for all in our group to grow and succeed;*

U - *you, the team member being the critical piece that we value; and*

S - *service as in servant leadership and service to our partners, customers, and peers.*

These are not perfect. It is hard to create a short list (respect, innovation, and many more deserve a place on the list), but you have to choose a few and make it clear what you stand for and then lead in that fashion.

One thing I tried to follow carefully was to not put myself in a situation where I was tempted to stray from my values or permit rumors to begin. Too many people in seats of power have allowed themselves to be caught in compromising situations. The situation might be temptations similar to what President Bill Clinton faced with Monica Lewinsky, or it may be where you are in a private setting and saying or doing something is taken out of context because there is no witness. For example, a doctor privately examining a patient or a teacher privately disciplining a student. You have to decide your values, design rules you will apply to uphold those values, and then do it.

Takeaway: It is important that people know what you as a leader stand for and what they can expect.

- Take stock of your personal values.
- Do you live by them?
- Develop a chart, documenting each of your values and how you live each one.
- Are values openly discussed in your organization? What values do your leaders manifest?

Figure 2: Doodle, Values

LESSON 8

REMEMBER WHO IS WATCHING

What you do speaks so loudly that I cannot hear what you say.
(Ralph Waldo Emerson)

This lesson applies equally to the business world and your personal life. As a leader, you have to "walk the talk." If you define and speak of values, you have to live them. If you expect your team or family to act or perform in certain way, you have to set the example.

In the workplace, people will be watching your every step: everything from your work ethic and everything you do in the office to how you handle yourself outside the office in your personal life. And if you strive to be a servant leader, the expectations are that you serve in all aspects of your life.

EXAMPLE

When my son was in third or fourth grade, he constructed a small picture frame made of Popsicle sticks. In the frame was a poem that, when I read it, stunned me. It brought all the adages such as "walk the talk" and "practice what you preach" to life.

A LITTLE FELLOW FOLLOWS ME

A careful man I want to be
A little fellow follows me.
I do not dare to astray
For fear he'll go self-same way.
I cannot once escape his eyes,
Whatever he sees me do he tries.
Like me he says he's going to be
The little chap who follows me.
He thinks that I am good and fine
Believes in every word of mine.
The base in me he must not see
The chap who follows me.
I must remember as I go
Thru summer's sun and winter's snow
I am building for the year to be
And that little chap who follows me.

This was in my office and now sits on my desk at home to remind me that not only are my children watching, but others are as well.

Takeaway: People are observing your behavior: at the office, on the road, away from work, and at home.

- What are the good behaviors you hope they observe?

- What are the worst of your behaviors that they might see?

- How can you minimize those bad behaviors in the future?

Figure 3: A Little Fellow Follows Me

48

LESSON 9

WRITE PERSONAL NOTES TO THE TEAM

Tell someone what a huge difference he or she made in your life. Reading your note will make a huge difference in that person's life . . . and in your relationship.
(Jeff Haden)

When you take the time to write notes, it speaks volumes as to the things you value. It says you value the team member as a person, as a note is a personal, intimate form of communication. It says that your time isn't too valuable to recognize others and that your priorities are in the right place. People appreciate something that their leadership has hand drafted and signed. A note has a sense of permanency.

This is not only true in the workplace but also with your family. Write a note to your mom/dad, thanking them for what they did for you; write a note to a professor, teacher, or coach who helped mold you; write a note to your young adult children about what you admire in them and your pride as their parent. Notes touch hearts.

EXAMPLE

Many strong leaders and famous persons have been handwritten note writers. Richard Branson and Jack Welch are famous CEOs who are prolific note writers. They encourage others to do the same. Now, we learn that Arnold Palmer was as well. On Monday mornings, Arnold Palmer, known as the King, would write a short note to the winners of weekend golf events—men and women, professionals and amateurs. He would write kind notes of understanding to players who just came up short of winning, as he had many times. He would write to tournament hosts and sponsors and volunteers. And he encouraged others to do it as well, most notably Jack Nicklaus. Arnold wrote his final notes a few weeks before his passing in the fall of 2016, with one note arriving in England two days after his death. The notes from the King touched people, and they have been saved and cherished over time.

The effect of personal notes really is surprising. If the CEO or Arnold Palmer took time to write you, you would save that. Though I wasn't a CEO or the King, people would tack up notes I wrote to them on their office or cube walls. They would take them home and show the notes to their family. Usually, the notes were about an extraordinary effort, a great success, leading a group, or recognition of the personal sacrifices the team member was making. Sometimes the subject was about how someone did an act of kindness for another member of our team. You can't make everyone rich, but you can make him or her feel rich with a sincere note of gratitude.

Takeaway: A personal note can make an impact.

- Have you ever been touched by a personal note? From whom?
- When in your role would it be appropriate to write notes?
- To whom should you consider writing? Family? Friends? Bosses? Team members?

LESSON 10

HELP PEOPLE CONNECT TO A LARGER SENSE OF PURPOSE

People want more than to just earn a living. They want meaning, they want purpose, they want to feel like their work is making a difference in the world."
(John Mackey, co-founder, Whole Foods)

When FedEx engaged a culture consultant to improve employee engagement, the consultants shared that the most positive cultures were found in organizations with a well-defined sense of purpose. The strongest positive cultures were in children's hospitals where everyone deeply wanted to see children heal and prosper. Public safety organizations have a strong sense of purpose, which ingrains itself into their culture. Many not-for-profit organizations tap the mission of serving, stewarding, and/or assisting to make the world, a community, or life better. In these cases, their team members strive to give a little more, care a little deeper, and propel the organization to deliver on its purpose.

When connected to a sense of purpose larger than the individual, team members are inspired. They relish the opportunity to be a part of making an impact. It fulfills their needs to achieve something substantial, give of themselves for the benefit of others, and be a part of something special. Author Robert Quinn documents this in his book *The Positive Organization: Breaking Free from Conventional Cultures, Constraints, and Beliefs* when he writes that the primary role of a leader is to connect people to a sense of purpose. He cites a famous example—USAA—where the purpose to serve those who have served our country is clear and palpable.[5]

EXAMPLE

As I have mentioned, team members at FedEx take great pride in being a part of something bigger than themselves. They feel as if they are part of something special. The origins of the company are so remarkable that not just employees but also the outside world consider them mythical. For example,

» Fred Smith wrote a paper in college at Yale University regarding a hub/spoke delivery system. *But did it really receive a "C"? Did it outline what Federal Express would ultimately find success delivering?*

» Mr. Smith flew to Las Vegas after a discouraging meeting with early financiers and won at the blackjack tables. *Did he really do that in desperation to cover payroll?*

» Cash flow in the early years was tight. *Did employees really have to hold their paychecks for weeks before they could be cashed? Did pilots really have to personally pay for jet fuel?*

Being a part of a team that created an industry, changed the world, and turned a noun into a verb is a special feeling.

The communications and public relations teams at FedEx have developed a set of programs that expands on the magic of the culture and connects people in multiple ways. There are a number of video streams on YouTube that help people connect to the mission and purpose of FedEx: videos on the humanitarian work following earthquakes in Nepal and Haiti strike at the heart; a video stream of team members going out of their way to save innocent people from floods, fires, and wrecks demonstrates the character of the team; a stream of "I Am FedEx" videos[6] highlights the uniqueness and individuality of team members all across the world; a series of videos featuring customers whose world has been opened by the "access" created by FedEx shows economic opportunities the company created.

Regardless of your organization and industry, look for how you make a difference in the world and connect your team to a larger purpose. Granted, it's easier if you work at Disney, St Jude's Children Hospital, or USAA. But all organizations are servicing a need or purpose. Find it and connect to it.

Takeaway: People want to feel they are making a difference and that they are part of something larger than themselves.[7]

- Do you help your team see their fit in the mission of the organization?

- How can you help connect the dots between their roles and the larger purpose of the organization?

LESSON 11

BE GRATEFUL

Gratitude is not only the greatest of virtues, but the parent of all others.
(Marcus Tullius Cicero)

For years the fields of religion and philosophy spoke of the importance of gratitude. Then psychologists and counselors began teaching the power of gratitude. Now, science in the form of neurological research is proving the impact of gratitude. Open a browser and search for gratitude, and the number of articles, studies, and testimonials is astounding! The research and observations show that people who regularly practice gratitude receive numerous benefits, including the following:

- Positive attitude, which generates more energy and focus

- Reduced level of stress, which helps manage stress-related illnesses

- Feelings of improved self-esteem and worth

- Increased willingness to help and serve others

To practice gratitude regularly, you do not need training or a life coach. It can begin with the simple thought of appreciation for something in your daily life. It can expand to planned moments of meditation with focus on things for which you are grateful. It can include journaling your gratitude. The practice can expand to having a gratitude partner with whom you share positive thoughts and events.

EXAMPLE

When FedEx Corporate Services engaged a consultant to do culture training, the concept of gratitude became a major area of focus. We were encouraged to speak openly of things for which we were grateful at work. We might start a meeting with a moment of gratefulness—verbally or silently. Try this at work or at home. Take a moment to reflect on what you and your companions are most grateful for that day, and share it aloud. It will lift spirits and inspire you when people speak of their parents and grandparents, a coach, or a teacher who made a difference in their life. They may speak of how the workgroup or the company was sympathetic to a loss or crisis in their life. Whatever is shared, it is positive and uplifting.

The consultant shared a tool: a continuum of attitudes from one extreme to the other. Predictably the low end of the continuum was depression, and the upper end was, drum roll please, gratitude. Using techniques such as the ones mentioned above and conscientiously focusing on gratitude can help you and your team members be more productive and drive engagement and commitment in both personal and professional lives.

Acknowledging the things for which you are grateful has lasting positive results. For many of us, the list is exhausting: health, freedom, education, abundance of food, choices, friends, safety and security, loved ones, and more. Unfortunately, there are others for whom the list is shorter. It's easy to say that regardless of where you are in life, there are things for which to be thankful. And indeed there are, but for those much further down the continuum, it's difficult to see past the immediate pain and be grateful. For those, it can be quite a journey through the continuum to reach gratitude. The servant leader can help along that journey. And in a full circle, the person being assisted is grateful for the help, and the servant is grateful to be able to serve and to grow through the act of service.

> **Takeaway: Gratitude is one the most powerful emotions in the human spirit. Regular expressions of gratitude can raise self-esteem and improve outlooks.**

- Do you practice gratitude on a regular basis? If not, how could you engrain it into your day or your work life?

- Start with a list of the main things you are grateful for in both your personal and professional life. Find time to reflect on those, and develop ways to express your gratitude.

- Studies on the impact of gratitude on wellbeing are powerful. Research a few of the articles, and develop a deeper understanding of the importance.

LESSON 12

SIX SPECIAL WORDS

Earning their respect begins the moment we recognize our mistakes and have the integrity and fortitude to utter the words, "I was wrong. I am sorry."
(Amy Rees Anderson)

E arlier I shared the lesson of owning your mistakes in the context of the business environment. The same concept applies to all dimensions in life, whether personal relationships, professional relationships, or even daily interactions with complete strangers. The servant leader in all walks of personal and professional life does not worry about how they will be perceived. They understand the power of humility and that serving others means accepting responsibility for mistakes they made. And the most powerful way to do that is to admit you were wrong. Thus six very special words: "I am sorry. I was wrong."

Beginning with "I am sorry" is the right place to start. The word *sorry* clearly indicates regret. But you cannot stop there. If you did, it can still be left up to conjuncture as to if you are sorry that someone else did something, someone misunderstood you, or if you are saying it in an empathetic and perhaps demeaning tone. Dr. Aaron Lazare writes in his book *On Apology* of the reasons that stopping with "I am sorry" is an inadequate apology.[8] The primary reason is there is no clear admission of responsibility. You have to continue and be specific. Using the first person of *I* makes it clear that you recognize the mistake and accept responsibility for the harm caused. "I was wrong" combined with "I am sorry" clearly indicates that you recognize you made a mistake, caused pain, regret the harm caused, and know that it was wrong. Going a step further and adding what you did wrong might even be better. That would eliminate any uncertainty.

EXAMPLE

There is a time in life when your children are too old to go to the church nursery during the service and too young to really concentrate on a sermon and retain much of the meaning. But occasionally a special sermon and speaker can make the message simple enough and interesting enough that both the adults and children retain it.

This happened one Sunday at our church in Orlando, First United Methodist of Orlando, where the conference bishop was visiting. The bishop delivered a sermon that we all could relate to and retain. It was the power of the six words: "I am sorry. I was wrong." As he told stories of people disappointing and hurting others, he explained the redemptive qualities of admitting our humanity and apologizing in a simple but sincere and correct manner. As he finished a story and came to the punch line, he would have us in unison call out, "I am sorry. I was wrong." We left the sanctuary, and the children spoke about the sermon. They got it. Years later we still speak of that sermon and the lesson it taught us. I know that we had plenty of occasions to practice it!

Takeaway: This lesson applies to all relationships in life. The servant leader, parent, spouse, sibling, friend, and coworker all need to do this. It is not a sign of weakness but of humility and strength.

- Do you voluntarily say the magic words—with sincerity—or do you have to be coerced?

- Can you think of a time you wish you had been more remorseful and timelier with your apology?

- Are there examples when someone else hurt your feelings by not apologizing or not apologizing with sincerity?

LESSON 13

GET OUT INTO THE FIELD WITH OPERATIONS AND CUSTOMERS

The most important thing that a commander can do is to see the ship from the eyes of the crew. (Commander D. Michael Abrashoff, USS Benfold)

Leaders have to stay connected with what it takes to make, deliver, and support their products or services. They have to get out of the office and see what is working and what needs attention. In doing so, they have the opportunity to be a servant leader by demonstrating their concern for the field/frontline employee. By giving their time to experience the daily activity of the frontline employee, they gain credibility. Hearing directly from the field and customers is invaluable and creates a connection with the workforce that is difficult to achieve from behind a desk. This is called "leading from the front."

The popular reality television show *Undercover Boss* exposes executive leaders to what their employees face day in and out. The "undercover" aspect was unnecessary, but the premise was good. In the show, not only did the executive get to see the processes in work, they also experienced it. If the tools or processes were poor, they could experience it. If the demands of the job were unreasonable, it was apparent. Ride-alongs with team members making the product or service are a proven technique that works two ways: it gives the executive perspective and input, and it gives the frontline team confidence that their leadership cares and is engaged.

Many corporations have programs where they require senior- and executive-level management to do customer calls and sponsor customer councils. The leaders support the sales team, which is great for the top line, but more importantly they get direct feedback from the customer as to industry changes, future trends, what the company could do better, and what the company can do to add more value.

EXAMPLE

There are a number of different techniques we used at FedEx to stay close to our people on the front line and to our customers. In the retail space, executives would make what is a traditional trip: surprise visits to stores. That would give them a great feel for customer experience and some exposure to the store staff. In office operations, leaders were expected to do "desk rides" with team members, doing functions such as revenue auditing or pricing. For field operations, we would go out of town to another market and spend days with field staff. Then we would submit observations back to a central program management desk for analysis to see if there were commonalities across regions and what should be addressed and changed. Our sales program assigned senior management to various markets across the country, and we would be in market four to six times a year doing customer calls and meetings.

All of these efforts enriched our knowledge of what customers and our team members needed. But it also gave each leader a chance to connect and serve our team members. We could listen and find things we could change to make their job better. We could knock down barriers or make a connection elsewhere within the corporation where someone else might be able to make a change. We could do little things for them like pick up and carry things to demonstrate we were not above helping. We could hear their sacrifices and then sincerely say "thank you" in person. We could spend time really getting to know them. These activities were as much about serving our team members as they were for us to gain information to do our jobs better.

In my particular case, I worked with the Columbus, Ohio, sales team for nearly seven years. Over seven years, even if you are in market only four or five times a year, you really get to know people. And that includes not only our team, but also the customers we were serving. Our people were wonderful, but so were our customers. When you get the privilege of working with people committed to the same goal, it's a pleasure.

Those trips to Columbus were many of my favorite experiences while working with FedEx. The FedEx team in the field is extraordinary. They have pride in what they do, they care about the customer, and they care for one another. Tom Peters famously wrote about FedEx in his books In Search of Excellence *and* A Passion for Excellence *where he described the lengths FedEx team members would go to deliver to a customer, including renting a helicopter to get beyond a snow jam!*

The FedEx team bleeds the company color of purple, and it shows. There are famous stories of Christmas Eve and Day deliveries. There are hundreds, if not thousands, of stories of FedEx drivers and couriers pulling over and performing acts of heroism to assist someone. Spending the time in the field with these people brought the stories to life. It made it rich, and it inspired you to do right by them: knock down a barrier, open a door to a potential account, solve a problem, go back to headquarters and fight to make their jobs easier. I'd like to think it gave them a degree of confidence that the people at headquarters did have their backs and really were in touch.

Takeaway: Leaders have to understand how and what their team does on a daily basis. They need to understand the customer experience. With that knowledge, they can then serve and make improvements for both the customer and the team.[9]

- Do you have insights into the efforts and processes your team members go through?
- Have you recently visited them in the field or conducted a desk ride?

Figure 4: Roadtrip

LESSON 14

SPEAK AND SEEK TRUTH

If you seek truth you will not seek victory by dishonorable means, and if you find truth you will become invincible. (Epictetus)

The 2016 presidential election introduced new concepts in truth and honesty: post-truth, alternative facts, and fake news, to name a few. In business, we referred to this as fear, uncertainty, and doubt (FUD). With these creations, it has become more difficult to find truth. Leaders who pursue a unilateral agenda often withhold critical information and propagate misinformation to energize their base of support while creating a cloud of confusion for others. As a result, it is difficult to parse the information and discern what the truth really is. Often, these are leaders in the sense that they hold authority and can issue directives. They are not leaders in the context of someone who is rallying people to achieve something for a greater good; they are trying to achieve their agenda at the expense of others. They are not leaders who seek truth but look to cloak the truth for their advantage. They are not leaders seeking to serve but to gain. Great leaders seek truth and are willing to hear truth.

In seeking truth, business leaders should focus on performance, not the emotions surrounding a matter. This depersonalizes the issue and encourages honest debate and exchange. The truth can be wonderful and glorious, but it can also be painful and concerning.

That is why it must be approached in a way to minimize the emotion, not allow falsehoods and personal attacks.

It is difficult to seek truth when people are driven by egos, narcissism, political motives, and personal ambition. The leader who insists on hearing the truth and allows truth to be told may not be popular. Those who believe in manipulation through half-truths and fake news will resist. Those upon whom the facts reflect less favorably have incentive to redirect focus through alternative facts, and redirection of focus often results in attacks on the leader.

EXAMPLE

When teams were at loggerheads and there was clear lack of cohesion, our executive would realign us with the importance of seeking truth in all we do. His advice was broad in scope: both personal and professional. He challenged us to make sure that we were honest and transparent in all aspects of our lives and we were true to our mission, whether at home or work. If we could find the structure and discipline to live within a values-based framework at home, we could find the structure to do so at work, and vice versa.

In the personal world, it was important to have a partner or spouse to hold you accountable to the truth. In the professional world, it was a mentor or colleague. Regardless of who it was, the person had to be empowered to speak truth with you. Tough love is often served with truth: reign in the ego; don't pretend your efforts aren't about you; don't slide in the world of alternative facts or post-truisms.

It was under this guidance that I continued to evolve toward servant leadership. I was beginning to understand the closed loop of truth: it was factual, with performance defined in terms of results and behavior, and non-emotional, to control for the tendencies to divert attentions through FUD (fear, uncertainty, and doubt). It also required our teams to be committed to our mission. You have to live to your values to set the behavior and deliver the results for the performance. You have to have discipline to manage FUD. To get the best performance from your teams, you need their hearts.

> **Takeaway: The leader serves the people to achieve the mission by seeking truth (rather than FUD) to ensure their success and by being true to their values.**

- What situations have you experienced when someone masked the truth?
- What were the consequences?
- In your organization, do leaders seek truth? How can you foster an environment that values and rewards the truth?

LESSON 15

NEVER GET IN THE WAY OF SOMEONE TRYING TO BETTER THEMSELVES

You can't keep good people down, and if they get a really good opportunity that you can't match, it's inevitable you're going to lose them. But that's the price you pay for having really outstanding people . . . Outstanding bosses who let their top talent leave developed reputations as launchpads. (Sydney Finkelstein)[10]

As a leader, you want a team of people that you can trust. You build them up and invest in them. You achieve successes and develop plans based on their abilities. In the process, they are growing and developing. Invariably, someone on the team will be ready to step up and move on to greater responsibilities or just desire a change. When that happens, as a leader you need to be supportive and encouraging. Your plans and the team may be impacted when someone leaves. But it's a healthy practice when embraced as positive for all and one that should encourage the rest of the tea

Some leaders value loyalty to such an extent that they interve discourage team members from moving on. The claim of lo not be the real motive—the leader often is trying to protect 67 of talent and perpetuate their success at the expense of the team. *Talent hoarding* is a counterproductive process. A recent study by the Institute for Corporate Productivity[11] found that half of managers surveyed admitted to talent hoarding, which holds employees back and is detrimental to the success of the whole. The study found that high-performing organizations were more than twice as likely to embrace movement of talent than lower-performing organizations. Further research is finding that letting "superstars" move internally and externally is good for the long-term health of organizations. It may smart immediately, but it creates the type of environment and reputation you want for the organization: one that recognizes and develops talent.

A servant leader strives to make their team and team members stronger. They want what is best for each. And they know that if their team members succeed, they as a leader have also succeeded.

EXAMPLE

As a leader, I had dozens of great people in my organization who were ready for more responsibilities. Over the course of my career, I learned to support people when they sought a change. That support would mean helping them consider and evaluate alternatives. When there were opportunities for promotion, I would help them assess the opportunity and how to pursue it. If someone wanted to go to graduate school, we would discuss the opportunity and whether the company could help or not. But the discussion was not about not going to school.

Likewise, if someone was thinking of leaving the company, as long as they were bettering themselves, I would be encouraging. If there was a path for them to stay and better themselves in an equal fashion, we would pursue that. Otherwise, I wanted what was best for them. Did it hurt our team when someone talented left? Yes, but a good leader has others ready to step up. Did it ~t my pride that they would choose to move to another part of ~mpany? Yes, but I refused to let my pride get in the way of ~ortunity.

A servant leader wants what is best for their people and must stop their ego from interfering.

Takeaway: Serving others means encouraging and helping them better themselves. A healthy organization promotes movement and growth.

- Does your organization advocate job rotation and growth?
- Are you or others in the organization *talent hoarders*?
- How can you make career movement a positive for both a valued team member and the organization?

CHAPTER TWO:

LEADERSHIP WISDOM

TWO: INTRODUCTION

The following chapter contains lessons learned from studying, observing, and trying to emulate the best traits of very good and great leaders. When you have a chance to work with great executives like Fred Smith and the FedEx executive team and board of director members at Fortune 500 companies, you can learn a lot. I tried to take notes about leadership styles and techniques used by these people. You can do the same wherever you are: identify leaders you admire, and observe them closely. Pattern yourself after them. Meanwhile, the process of leading will give you experience—and experience is a powerful teacher. You may learn from your victories, but you should definitely learn from mistakes and any failures you incur. A number of these lessons come from my firsthand experience.

As my responsibilities at FedEx expanded, I went from leading a team, to a group of teams, to a full organization of approximately four hundred people. Then I had the opportunity to serve as the chief information officer of one our operating companies, FedEx Freight. This experience gave me a flavor of the role a C-level executive plays in setting strategy and vision. The experience was rich with decisions and learnings but was cut short with a call back to the mothership of FedEx and a much larger role: to be responsible for the portfolio of technology solutions supporting our customers, including ecommerce technology. Ultimately the role would mean leading a team of fifteen hundred people concentrated in six cities in the US and roughly a thousand contractors around the world. In this role, we had global responsibilities for the technology supporting the FedEx revenue stream, at the time $40 billion, and the pressure to keep FedEx on pace or ahead of the competition.

This is not the largest job in the world or the one with the direst of consequences. But often it was called the "toughest job at FedEx" because you were trying to make everyone happy but also keep the shipments coming in and the revenue flowing. It was important enough that a section of the annual 10-K SEC filing detailed the work our team produced.[12] The competition was always doing something new, and the company was always asking for more and more. If we stumbled, it meant lost revenue, and in some cases, lost customers. Our shipping services were embedded directly into the supply chains of our customers. If customers could not ship, it was a disaster; they might take their business elsewhere. Problems where we lost revenue or worse, customers, affected the livelihood of the sales team and all the operations team members. We were a critical link in the chain of the company's success and in turn, the career opportunities of our employees. Truthfully, because of the tightly integrated system network, which is FedEx, many groups had similar levels of risk to the operations. But most of those were internal operations who did not have to respond to competitive pressures and consumers' rising expectations regarding technology. They were not as visible to the external world.

To meet the pressures of increasing demand, changes in technology such as mobile computing and the "law of rising expectations," competition with UPS, and acquisitions, we had to have all our people fully engaged and committed to our mission. In this role, I believed my job was to understand the strategy and vision from the executive team, work with my business partners to develop a roadmap to support the mission, and then execute the mission. This meant being a servant leader who would help the team succeed. All my experiences to date had sculpted me for the role I was being asked to undertake.

This was actually the second time I was asked to serve in this role; in both instances, we had fallen behind the competition and needed to turn around our capabilities. Both times, we had to regain the confidence of our sales and operations teams and deliver a superior product. It was hard work to catch up and get ahead. With the help and guidance of great business partners on the product marketing side of the house, we changed our trajectory and delivered.

After the first time, I moved on to the chief information officer (CIO) job at FedEx Freight. A few years later, I was asked to come back to this role but in an expanded capacity and right the ship again. The second effort was just as hard as the first but as rewarding in our success. The learning from that effort was to never again let up once you get ahead. It takes so much energy and effort to catch up and build a lead that you cannot afford to lose focus and coast. As I would say until the day I left the company, "We worked too hard to get to this point. Do not take your foot off the accelerator."

The lessons in this chapter are gleaned from those years of leading at a senior level at FedEx. However, they are not intended for management (frontline, middle, senior, or executive level) only. As we will discuss, leaders do not have to be in management; they can be individual contributors. Our organization was blessed with many leaders who were not in management and did not seek a title. They were truly selfless leaders who cared for the mission and their teammates. We could not have achieved what we did without them.

A note: Not all leaders are servant leaders. Nevertheless, the lessons still apply, as they are intended to make the leader the best they can be.

LESSON 16

NOT EVERYTHING IS WIN-WIN, OR EVEN WIN-LOSE

A compromise is when we are all equally unhappy. (Anonymous)

I t is always a great moment when you achieve a win-win result in almost any professional endeavor. It's magical when everyone can get most of what they wanted. Too often we are exposed to win-lose situations: sporting matches, competing for a recruit against another company, sometimes budget trade-offs within the corporation, or promotions. But there are times when you may end up in a lose-lose scenario and euphemistically call it a compromise. These are times when you can't get majority satisfaction, and neither can the other side. After hours or days or sometimes even months, a lose-lose scenario is the best outcome. You compromise to a point where *no one* is happy. It's a vital arrow in the quiver for the leader who has to negotiate in a very bad situation.

EXAMPLE

The situation was plagued with errors by both sides. We went over and over the details, agreeing that both sides made mistakes but failing to agree if one set of the errors was more damaging or egregious than another set of errors. We agreed to take a few days' break to see if there were any additional details that would shed light on the root cause of the problem. But there were not, and we went through the litany of mistakes again and again. There was no win-win here. Both sides were playing for win-lose, hoping the other would capitulate. But neither would. We would reconvene tomorrow.

That night my colleagues and I developed a strategy to call the other side's bluff: we'll offer to go to binding arbitration, which would guarantee a win-lose verdict. So the next day, after spending hours confirming that the facts had not changed, we made the offer of arbitration. After a recess to allow the other side to consider the possibility, they returned with a proposal. So neither of us would run the risk of losing, they said, let's find a position where we both are equally miserable. In effect, they were proposing a lose-lose scenario. There would be no winner. Neither side would get anywhere near what they felt they deserved. We felt our case was strong, but legal counsel reminded us that in arbitration, the human factor sometimes plays a role. We would be best to end this battle and accept a lose-lose scenario.

Takeaway: Compromise is a critical arrow to carry in your quiver.

- Do you see leaders in your organization that always try to steamroll their way to win-lose resolutions? Are they admired?

- In what situations would you need to seek a compromise—at work and at home?

LESSON 17

THERE CAN BE NO PLACE FOR WORKPLACE VIOLENCE, HARASSMENT, OR DISCRIMINATION

A respectful workplace is free from unlawful discrimination and harassment, but it involves more than compliance with the law. It is a work environment that is free of inappropriate or unprofessional behavior and consistent with 3M's ethics and values—a place where everyone can do his or her best and where people are free to report workplace concerns without fear of retaliation or reprisal.
(3M Code of Conduct)

T here can be *no* tolerance for workplace violence, harassment, or discrimination. Period. The workplace must be a safe place for all to practice their craft without fear of violence. It must be a place free of hatred and harassment for all to feel free to contribute. It must be free of discrimination so all have opportunities and can contribute to the mission of the organization while fulfilling their individual potential. As a manager or leader, this is one of the most important responsibilities you have: to ensure the workplace is a safe and fair environment. And remember that what happens at work often sets the tone for life outside of work.

You must champion diversity. You have to set the example. Diversity is important for a number of reasons. First, it enables the contribution of multiple perspectives that enriches strategy and policy debates. Second, it champions the opportunity for the development of resources that have been systematically denied opportunities in the past. Third, diversity sends a message that within your organization, all are valued. At one point in my career, I had nine direct reports, and eight of the nine were female and/ or minorities. They not only brought the appropriate qualifications and skills to their jobs, but they added unique perspectives to the organization.

With respect to workplace safety and violence, again, there can be no tolerance. If anything suggests there is a risk, you must take action and engage security, human resources, and legal immediately. Part of being a leader requires that you care for the well-being of your team, and you need to proactively think about scenarios where their safety may be jeopardized. When people must work late, how do you ensure that they are secure and comfortable? How do you ensure they can get home safely? Do you have procedures for natural disasters, such as a tornado, where you can account for everyone? What other scenarios might apply to your organization?

Harassment can take multiple forms, and as a leader, you must make people feel comfortable coming to management—via an open-door policy—to report harassment of any kind. You cannot be in every hallway, meeting, or conversation to witness harassing behavior. So you must create an environment where people feel comfortable to step forward. It is incumbent on you as the leader to create that environment of trust so people can come forward without fear of retribution. Otherwise, a subculture of fear and intimidation will develop. Once individuals do come forward, you have to investigate and take appropriate action. That action can be discipline up to and including termination, demotion, or coaching. But the behavior must be modified.

One particular form of harassment is sexual harassment. As Marianne Cooper wrote in *The Atlantic*, "What determines whether or not a company is tolerant of sexual harassment? In a word, leadership."[13] The leader of an organization sets the tone and example for others to follow. People in leadership positions have a degree of authority and power that can be used in an abusive fashion. All who are given authority must establish values and boundaries to ensure they do not abuse their perceived privilege. I was extremely careful not to put myself in situations that could lead to temptations or presumptions. That meant being very careful about where and when I would have one-on-one meetings or meals with women who worked for me. To make sure that this never becomes an issue, one must consciously define his or her values and set personal practices and policies to live to those values.

EXAMPLE

When the leader of one of our teams was bullying their staff, none of the affected personnel filed a complaint. But word leaked that the leader was condescending and belittling the staff. For whatever reason, the staff did not feel free to raise it to my level, and they did not have confidence that the situation would be remedied. After interviewing all the staff and other support personnel, I could piece together a pattern of behavior that required modification. Coaching and discipline changed the behavior. The next step was to make sure that everyone in our organization knew they worked in an environment that would not tolerate that type of behavior.

EXAMPLE

After decades of abuse, sexual harassment in the workplace has been exposed and hundreds of cases of legislators, executives, celebrities, ministers, professors, judges, and others perpetuating the abuse have been documented. Most, though not all of the abusers, have lost their positions. Many organizations such as Fox News, Amazon Studios, and Uber have had to purge their leadership teams and deconstruct their culture to eradicate the behavior.

Takeaway: As a leader, you must make it clear that violence, harassment, and discrimination will not be tolerated in your organization.

- Have you witnessed any of these things? If so, what action did you or other leaders take?

- How do you ensure your team knows they may come to you and safely share any concerns regarding violence, harassment, or discrimination?

- Are you prepared for a safety-related incident at work?

- How do you feel about people in positions of authority abusing their power through harassment?

LESSON 18

WHEN TIMES ARE TOUGH, BE POSITIVE BUT HONEST

Your good old days are still ahead of you . . . (Sam Levenson)

T his lesson comes from years of observing one of the great business leaders in America, Fred Smith. Business cycles are inevitable, and if you are in business long enough, you will see slowdowns and recessions, such as 1981–83, 1992–94, and 2001–02. Unfortunately, we also witnessed more than a typical recession in '08–'09; it was a man-made implosion of markets and resulted in the Great Recession. With experience and pattern recognition, a strong leader knows that cyclical downturns are cyclical and, in many cases, actually present an opportunity. They may express their concern in internal meetings, but to the workforce they turn positive. The team needs their wisdom, calm and steady hand, and the promise that they will prevail. It is a time to be realistic and honest but positive and visionary. That is what Mr. Smith did. He promised the FedEx community we would do what we needed to during the hard times but we would also use this as an opportunity to improve. We would emerge stronger and more competitive. This was clearly explained in the FedEx Corporation 2010 Annual Report.

When times are tough, people need their leaders to increase communication and be honest with them as to the situation but encouraging as to the future. Silence in a tough time allows rumor and fear to flourish. So the great leader steps up with a positive attitude, communicating frequently, admitting the gravity of the situation, describing the sacrifices needed, and motivating the team to persevere.

EXAMPLE

Great examples from the twentieth century demonstrate this. President Franklin D. Roosevelt became president during the Great Depression and immediately used communication via his first inaugural address and then later through "Fireside Chats" to reassure the nation:

> This is preeminently the time to speak the truth, the whole truth, frankly and boldly. Nor need we shrink from honestly facing conditions in our country today. This great Nation will endure as it has endured, will revive and will prosper. So, first of all, let me assert my firm belief that the only thing we have to fear is fear itself . . .

> We face the arduous days that lie before us in the warm courage of the national unity; with the clear consciousness of seeking old and precious moral values; with the clean satisfaction that comes from the stern performance of duty by old and young alike. We aim at the assurance of a rounded and permanent national life.

Roosevelt would continue with the communication strategy during his "Fireside Chats," reassuring the nation that progress was being made.

Winston Churchill's oratory to the British people during the Battle of Britain is another classic example:

> Do not let us speak of darker days; let us rather speak of sterner days. These are not dark days; these are great days—the greatest days our country has ever lived; and we must all thank God that we have been allowed, each of us according to our stations, to play a part in making these days memorable in the history of our race. Never give in, never give in, never, never, never, never—in nothing, great or small, large or petty—never give in except to convictions of honor and good sense.

> . . . the Battle of Britain is about to begin. Upon this battle depends the survival of Christian civilization. Upon it depends our own British life, and the long continuity of our institutions and our Empire. The whole fury and might of the enemy must very soon be turned on us. Hitler knows that he will have to break us in this Island or lose the war. If we can stand up to him, all Europe may be free and the life of the world may move forward into broad, sunlit uplands. . . . Let us therefore brace ourselves to our duties, and so bear ourselves that, if the British Empire and its Commonwealth last for a thousand years, men will still say, "This was their finest hour."

> We shall defend our island, whatever the cost may be, we shall fight on the beaches, we shall fight on the landing grounds, we shall fight in the fields and in the streets, we shall fight in the hills; we shall never surrender.

A few years later, General Dwight D. Eisenhower was appointed supreme commander of the Allied forces in Europe. Eisenhower also understood the importance of the leader never showing doubt or pessimism:

> I firmly determined that my mannerisms and speech in public would always reflect the cheerful certainty of victory—that any pessimism and discouragement I might ever feel would be reserved for my pillow.
>
> Optimism and pessimism are infectious and spread more rapidly from the head down more than in any other direction.
>
> Without confidence, enthusiasm, and optimism in the command, victory would scarcely be obtainable.

EXAMPLE

There are great examples in business as well. When 9/11 crippled the airline business, Southwest Airlines CEO James Parker did not follow the lead of other airlines with layoffs and cost reductions; instead he announced on 9/14 that Southwest would retain all employees and begin an employee profit sharing program. His optimism and quick response reassured the Southwest team and motivated them to deliver even better service during a turbulent time.

EXAMPLE

During the Great Recession, 3M's CEO, George Buckley, went beyond communication and transparency to assure employees that he had faith in them and that they would not be blamed for things beyond their control—such as the state of the economy.

EXAMPLE

In the world of sports, great coaches take adversity and turn it into opportunity. Indulge me as I write of two examples from college basketball, which just so happen to involve my alma mater, Duke University. In 1992 Duke was playing the University of Kentucky for a berth in the Final Four. Duke was the defending national champion and number one ranked team. They were trying to accomplish a repeat championship for the first time since the great John Wooden UCLA teams. The Duke-UK game was a fiercely contested game, which was coming down to a nail biting conclusion. Kentucky scored on a miraculous shot with 2.1 seconds left to take the lead. Duke called time out. As his players returned to the bench, Duke's Coach Mike Krzyzewski's (Coach K's) first words were, "We are going to win this game." They had to traverse the length of the court and score in 2.1 seconds. But Coach K was positive. The rest is history. Grant Hill threw a perfect pass to Christian Laettner, who in turn hit a perfect jump shot.

In 2001 Coach K was still leading Duke University's men's basketball team—the top ranked team in the nation. But disaster struck in the last week of the regular season. His star center, Carlos Boozer, broke his foot, and with that injury, the hopes for a Blue Devil national championship seemed lost. But, within a day, Coach K went to his team and told them that if they believed in him and his plan, they would win the national championship. They had three days before their next game, and he was going to use that time to completely revamp the team's style of play to make up for the loss of their center. He was adamant that if they committed, they would win the national championship. The team believed, their change in style baffled opponents, and through his leadership, Coach K had dealt with adversity and converted it into opportunity. And, yes, they did win the national championship.

In my own career, we often faced challenges, and when they arose, my strategy was to get out in front of the team and discuss it with them. I might not be able to give the team specifics on the courses of action, but communicating and reassuring them that the executive team—the best executives in the business—were working on the issues helped. It helped them have faith in our executive team and hope for the future. I would be honest about the situation and positive regarding the outcome. Whether it was 9/11, the recession of '01–'02, or the Great Recession of '08–'09, we would over communicate (but not share confidential plans) to assure our team that we would emerge stronger and better from the current situation. And then we all worked together to make that reality happen.

Takeaway: When people are faced with adversity, they look to a leader for reassurance and direction.

- In your career, have you witnessed times when leaders have had to reassure the team that better times will come?

- How about in your personal life?

- What can you do in your role to provide positive leadership in difficult times?

LESSON 19

WHEN TIMES ARE GOOD, PUSH AND CHALLENGE YOUR TEAM

If you are in a downturn, help put out the fire. If you are in status quo, start a fire. If you are in an upturn, pour fuel on the fire. (Bill Hybels)

T his is a corollary to "When Times are Bad." In that lesson, leaders need to be positive but honest with their teams when times are bad. In this lesson, the leader needs to leverage good times and challenge the team so complacency does not set in.

When you are running with the wind, it's easy to let up and coast a bit. Research shows a benefit of five percent efficiency gain with a ten mile per hour wind at your back. If you dial back and ride the wind, you have gained nothing against the clock. If you maintain effort, you gain five percent. If you leverage the wind and push a bit, you are gaining a greater return. Also remember that the course, like an economy, can turn back into the wind. Running into the wind, you have to exert eight percent more effort to maintain pace. So "make hay while the sun shines" and the wind is at your back.

In good times, "sharpen the saw," as Covey's *Seven Habits of Highly Effective People* suggests. This is a time to be improving as a leader and improving as an organization.

EXAMPLE

As the economy would swing into an expansion, our CEO would launch a series of initiatives to make sure everyone was on their game and no complacency would occur. Quality initiatives, productivity programs, BHAGs (Big Hairy Audacious Goals), organization changes, and innovation challenges would be fired at us. The comforting leader—who in the downturn would reassure everyone that we would be fine and gain from a downturn—would shift into a demanding leader who wanted to maximize the opportunities before us.

Some leaders wait for a burning platform to make a major change. Others are proactive and see that in good times, when everything seems to be going well and change doesn't seem necessary, it is the time to strike. Time to go from good to better, better to best.

Takeaway: A true leader knows when to push the team and expand a lead. Don't coast when in a competitive situation.

- How can you challenge your team in good times to be even better?

- Are there examples you have witnessed that can serve to inspire you and the team?

LESSON 20

ALLOW HONEST FEEDBACK— A NO HINT ZONE

Every organization should tolerate rebels who tell the emperor he has no clothes.
(General Colin Powell)

There are times when you need to hear the truth. People need to be free to say what is working and what is not—as long as they keep it objective and not personal. This can be achieved in a number of ways. One way is where a team comes together to debrief after a procedure or mission is complete, using the concept of "leaving rank at the door." In other words, everyone is free to speak, and there are no judgmental hierarchies in the discussion. This is a great technique to continually improve in a high-performance environment or to identify true root causes for systematic failures.

Another method is to permit open dialogue by creating *judgment free zones* or *no hint zones*. These figurative zones allow subordinates to invoke the zone in order to speak freely without judgment or retribution. In organizations with powerful hierarchical cultures, this is a very useful technique.

Author Malcolm Gladwell relates the story of the crash of Korean Airlines Flight 801 in his book *Outliers*.[14] The point of the story is how culture influences behavior and how sometimes the consequences can be disastrous. In this case, the Korean hierarchal culture of being deferential to elders and superiors inhibited the sharing of vital information from navigator to pilot. Specifically, the plane was in extremely poor weather and attempting to make a visual landing. When the navigator could determine from the radar they were heading into a mountain, he could only hint to the pilot that a change in course was needed. His hint is what is referred to as *mitigated speech*. Unfortunately, the pilot did not pick up on the subtleties of the navigator's mitigated or indirect speech and flew the plane into the mountain, killing all on board.

Mitigated speech is the byproduct of behavior documented through Geert Hofstede's seminal research in power distance index (PDI).[15] PDI is a way to measure the extent to which less powerful members of a particular culture accept and expect that power is distributed unequally within the hierarchy. Organizations with strong command structures and cultures often have high PDIs. The possibility of accidents, mistakes, and disasters occurring in high PDI organizations is strong. As a result, the health care industry has invested in training and procedures to minimize risk by lowering PDI and empowering team members to speak up. Teams, whether in the operating room or on rounds, are empowered to speak and stop a procedure if there is doubt. The military allows subordinates to request, "Permission to speak, sir." They have debrief sessions with no rank. While not completely mistake proof, these are steps in the right direction.

The business world is not immune to this. Organizations with high PDI have an inherent communication barrier that must be remediated. In such organizations, executives, managers, or leaders share a perception of unequal status with their subordinates. This means subordinates are trained to salute and execute orders and not question or share information contrary to orders. As a result, mistakes can be made.

To avoid this, leaders and managers can work with their teams to make sure they understand that sharing and speaking out, especially in times of trouble, are an accepted practice. Also, make the distance between team member and manager small so the manager is accessible. And making sure everyone understands that they all share the same goals makes it clear that speaking up to avoid a mistake is in everyone's interest.

EXAMPLE

The US Navy Blue Angels are a precision flying team that astounds with their formations, stunts, and nerves. Six fighter jets fly just feet apart while performing challenging maneuvers and stunts. In fact, in their "diamond formation," they fly just eighteen inches apart. This requires incredible teamwork, concentration, trust, and discipline. After every team flight, training, or performance, the pilots debrief. As they enter the debrief room, they leave their rank at the door. During the debrief they must be able to speak truth and not be afraid of hierarchical judgment. The debriefs strengthen trust and continually improve their performance.

EXAMPLE

We borrowed the concept in debrief sessions where we would review product launches or system implementations. When we left rank at the door, everyone was empowered to speak up and share their observation or suggestion. These became very powerful, continuous improvement processes.

Similarly, we found opportunities to practice the no hint zone or judgment free zone concepts. We had a situation where we were pushing major culture changes through our division. But, we had not adequately communicated or sold the changes to the rank and file. We were losing their commitment and discretionary effort. As managers, we could see the turmoil, but we did not feel empowered to question the wisdom of the changes. When employee engagement surveys were conducted, executive management could see the damage that had been done. We went immediately into damage control mode. Meanwhile, executive management shared the Gladwell story and committed to change culture to reduce the PDI. We were now officially encouraged to "pull the cord" if necessary to avoid a train wreck.

There are times when, in the middle of an operation or a meeting, you have to "pull the cord." But there are other situations where you can share information with a higher-ranking person in private. If the situation could wait, I would do that and speak to the issue during a private meeting. I start out invoking the *no hint zone*, which in effect is similar to saying, "Permission to speak, sir." In the *no hint zone*, I could speak openly and honestly without repercussion.

Meanwhile, I told my team the same thing: they could come to me and invoke the *no hint zone* and speak freely. As I have coached others, this is a lesson I believe all should practice. They can work this practice upstream with their boss and downstream with their teams. The goal is to get honest feedback and avoid flying into a mountain.

Takeaway: Allow a time and place for honest feedback. Encourage people to speak openly of major concerns to avoid surprises.

- How could you implement a *no hint zone* or a *judgment free zone*?
- Read chapter seven in Gladwell's *Outliers* with your team. Discuss how the two plane crashes described apply to your organization.

LESSON 21

PROFIT IS NOT A FOUR-LETTER WORD

A rising tide lifts all boats. (Anonymous)

OK, *profit* isn't a four-letter word. It may be six letters, but to our team members, they would sometimes bristle at the constant drive to increase earnings per share (EPS) instead of making investments they deemed important. They would cite the corporate culture of People—Service—Profit with "people first" being the driver of service and profit. They were concerned that profit was becoming the focus at the expense of people. Specifically, the belief was that the benefits of profitability were not being shared proportionally with the team members in terms of higher compensation and professional development. Profits were going up and team members were asked to do more and more, but they perceived they were receiving less and less. Thus *profit* was viewed by some as a four-letter word.

In this situation, leadership has to step up and communicate the importance of profitability as it applies to investors, lenders, team members, and the corporation's ability to support community and corporate responsibility activities. Simplistically, investors require a certain return on their investment. Lenders require that certain covenants be met to ensure corporate viability in order to protect their positions. Team members need equipment, training, and compensation. And profitability is important to funding community and corporate responsibility programs. In planning, if you can get to the bottom line with more than what the investor requires, there is opportunity to go back and invest more in team members, equipment, training, and corporate responsibility programs and still achieve the investor's expectations.

When times are tight, the ability to get to that acceptable bottom line may require tradeoffs in investment strategies and what can be shared to team members. Those are the times when it seems profit is drowning out the benevolent side of the culture. Thus these are the times to explain that profit isn't evil. The more we can drive towards the bottom line, the more opportunity everyone will have as we can reinvest some of that into the people, equipment, future, and special services of the company.

EXAMPLE

In the commercial world, the profit motive sometimes drowns out other senses of purpose. Asking team members to reach deep for a pure monetary purpose appeals to some, but most team members want to know they are making a difference in something or for someone. To do this, you have to step back and look at what it is your organization provides and how your team fits into that overall picture.

Working at FedEx, we could always anchor ourselves to a set of noble purposes that superseded the profit motive. For example, FedEx created time definite access to global markets and in doing so created opportunity for individuals, companies, and consumers to fulfill dreams. The outstanding overnight service moved life-saving shipments to people in dire needs. We made new business models possible. Furthermore, the company often responded to natural disasters as or nearly as fast as first responders. FedEx would move supplies, medicine, food, and more to impacted regions all over the world. Those were noble causes that we could all be proud to be a part of.

For our team, our role was to empower the operational teams with services and capabilities. When we would launch a new initiative, which was to drive up revenue or reduce costs, we would step back and talk about how this project would contribute to the sense of purpose. In some cases, we opened new markets, which provided opportunities for people that they never had before. In other cases, we were contributing to the bottom line, and that in turn made sure the company could make a difference in people's lives when disaster struck. Working hard to increase profitability helped FedEx satisfy investors but also make a difference in the world. Profit was not a four-letter word.

For team members who were motivated primarily by monetary rewards, our leadership team also was able to provide a sliding scale of proportional sharing of profit if we could meet or exceed ambitious earnings per share (EPS) goals. Brilliantly, this simplified the algebra for the team. If we drove enough to the bottom line, we were able to contribute to reinvestment in our people and businesses.

Takeaway: Help your team understand the importance of good stewardship and fiscal management. Growth and profitability are critical to a commercial enterprise.

- Does your organization "tighten the belt" and manage expenses at times to meet or improve bottom-line results? When that occurs, does training, business travel, bonuses, pay raises, and refreshment of equipment get delayed or reduced?

- How can you frame the expense controls in a positive fashion for your team?

- Are there ways you or the team can not only accept and support the controls but also demonstrate commitment to the end goals of the organization?

LESSON 22

IT'S OKAY NOT TO HAVE ALL THE ANSWERS

There is nothing wrong with making mistakes and not having all the answers, as long as we are willing to admit this and strive for personal betterment. Those who think they know it all have no way of finding out that they don't. (Leo Buscaglia)

When you are the leader of a group, it feels like everyone expects you to have all the wisdom and knowledge to solve any and all problems that arise. You sit at the head of the table, and the head of the table is reserved for the wisest person in the group: patriarch, matriarch, guru, or some other form of omnipotent leader. For sure! Early in your leadership journey, you may feel you have to have the answers. But, with time, you will realize that it is okay not to have the answers. The wisdom you must have is to know when to admit you don't know something and to seek advice. It is not a sign of weakness. It's a good leadership practice.

Great leaders also understand how to use the art of asking questions to help them find answers. Some leaders may have the Socratic wisdom to ask penetrating questions that reveal the answer. Most, however, have learned through their experiences when to probe, the tone to use, and when to pull back. They ask, *why? what are the alternatives? what are the barriers? how can I help? have other opinions been sought? what are the risks? how do we prove something works or is true?* and more.

When you ask questions, do not cross-examine. Ask open-ended questions with the intent to seek input. Ask, and then listen. If team members get flustered or uncomfortable, reassure them: you don't have all the answers either.

EXAMPLE

For a long time, I was convinced that sitting at the head of the table meant I should be as wise as King Solomon. No matter the issue, I should be able to see the answer. And it wore heavy on me. Then I started to observe strong leaders in our company and how they operated. They would listen rather than talk. They would ask questions and request alternatives. They would then ask for recommendations to accompany alternatives. Sometimes they would have to make a decision with only twenty or thirty percent of the relevant information. But most of the time, they made sure they had the majority of the information. And from observing them, I realized it was okay for me to not have every answer.

If you agree with me that the role of a leader is to motivate people to achieve a common objective, then the most important things a leader must do are define the objective, build a team, motivate the team, and remove obstacles so the team can succeed. Of course, along the way, issues must be faced and decisions made. But the leader doesn't have to have all the answers. The leader can rely on the team for insight, recommendations, and assistance in making decisions.

Takeaway: You don't have to have answers to the problems your team faces. The expectation is that you will ask wise questions, seek guidance, and find answers.

- Have you seen any effective leaders ask questions and direct a process to find an answer to a problem?
- What techniques did the leader use? How did people react?
- Have you had to do this in your role?

LESSON 23

COMMUNICATE, COMMUNICATE, COMMUNICATE

If communication is not your top priority, all of your other priorities are at risk.
(Bob Aronson)

There is a great leadership development exercise where a person is blindfolded and given piecemeal instruction to complete a complex task. After floundering for a while, the blindfold is removed, and they can see what the end goal was. If while blindfolded they had been given a description of the end result, they could have made sense of the haphazard instructions and worked to the goal.

Team members are too often blindfolded and asked to work from piecemeal instruction. They ask, *what is the vision? where are we going? what is about to happen?* All are common reactions from people whose future and livelihood is in your hands. The more you can share with people, the better their buy-in and performance. Of course, there are times when confidentiality requires holding things close to the chest, but when possible, explaining the why, what, and where with the team makes a more engaged workforce.

EXAMPLE

There are times when things are tight, and in the vacuum of silence, rumors circulate. Over a long career, we experience the cyclical nature of the economic swings. During those tough times, doubling down on communications with video, brown bag lunches, town halls, and other media demonstrates a care and respect for the workforce.

In other times, transformation or change creates angst, and the questions of vision and direction arises. The team needs to understand the rationale for the changes and then the vision of future state accompanied by the description of the journey to get there. This takes time and energy, but communication is critical.

EXAMPLE

Our team had a communications specialist who helped us make sure we had a constant flow of information. Playing off my last name of Zanca, we created a series of Z-communications. We used Z-mails for short announcements and recognitions. Brown bag lunches to discuss what was on the minds of our team members were called Zunches. Our format was simple. While everyone ate, I'd talk for about ten minutes and then answer questions for thirty minutes. Before availability of bandwidth for streaming, we created ZDs (CDs with multiple types of content). Later we would stream Z-tube content instead of a CD. We'd produce different segments featuring a guest or highlighting a specific team or location. Town halls were regularly scheduled in all our locations (six cities in the United States) with silly trivia questions interspersed to break up what might be monotony with the reward of a trip to the "priZe bar." We always included plenty of time for open discussion. It was a very comprehensive program to be as transparent as possible.

There are also times when you have to clarify and provide transparency on an individual level. Sometimes the corporate world can take an unexpected turn, and someone can be caught in the turbulence. For example, a sudden hiring freeze can leave a candidate for a position in limbo. If the candidate is an existing team member looking to change roles, they may feel exposed with their current manager; or maybe they were relocating. A project cancellation can upend numerous people's plans. When your team or a team member gets caught in corporate reorganizations, freezes, and other general uncertainties to which they are not privy, you need to go out of your way to communicate and be as transparent as possible. Explain to them that they have done nothing wrong. Reassure them of their value to the company, and explain as much as you can as to why something happened. Many times the reason for a change in strategy or direction has not been announced, but the repercussions are being felt. In that case, be as honest as you can. Your team member may not like it, but they can respect you for being honest. I personally experienced this numerous times on both sides: leader and team member.

Takeaway: As a leader, it is important to have an effective form of communication for your team. The form will vary depending on your personality, style, location, and role.

- What communications needs does your team have?
- What has worked in the past?
- Are there additional forms or frequency of communication that is needed?
- Are there leaders in your organization that are highly effective communicators from whom you can learn?

LESSON 24

CAREFULLY DECIDE WHEN TO ASK FORGIVENESS RATHER THAN PERMISSION

Do what is right, not what you think the high headquarters wants or what you think will make you look good. (General Norman Schwarzkopf)

S trong leaders initiate action. They see an opportunity or challenge, envision the solution, and motivate people to follow them to resolution.

Sometimes the opportunity or challenge may be on the borderline between two organizations. Or it may be in a gray space. It may require changing priorities and redirecting resources. These are the times where, as a leader, you have to ask yourself if you should proceed or ask permission and wait. If the opportunity is fleeting, waiting is a poor choice. If the action is clearly the right thing to do, taking initiative and asking forgiveness is a better answer.

As a leader you need to have a framework to make these decisions. You should not choose to deviate from your given path just because you see a squirrel. Usually, others are counting on you to complete the journey on that path, and they can be exposed by your diversion. Weigh the impact to the organization before you decide. Also consider your motivation to proceed without permission: are you trying to circumvent policies or steadfast rules? Have you been specifically told "no," or is there a policy that specifically forbids the action? If so, understand the consequences for that choice.

When you believe it to be appropriate to take action, move with conviction. Don't second-guess your choice, as you are committed at this point. Press ahead and complete what you set out to do. Then ask forgiveness. Hopefully, it's not forgiveness for doing something wrong. It's forgiveness for not asking permission.

EXAMPLE

Leaders not only make decisions such as when to ask permission and when to not, they also empower their teams to do the same. Leaders do not impose their control at all times; when necessary, they allow their team members to make decisions without their specific permission. In the Marine Corp leadership model, it's critical that everyone engaged with an operation understands the commander's intent. Then, when individuals have to make decisions, they are not constrained by having to ask permission. They are empowered to act within the commander's intent.

EXAMPLE

At FedEx, we had a procedure where, in a crisis, such as our website or shipping systems being down, our response team was empowered to make decisions. They did not have to call their bosses or ask me for approval to take a specific action. They were empowered to do what was necessary to restore service to the quality standards we had previously defined. Sometimes that had consequences for other parts of the business or other customers; sometimes that meant acquiring and deploying assets using approval exception processes. After the fact, it was our leadership team's job to explain the actions taken and why it was necessary, document the exception process justification—in a manner of speaking—and ask forgiveness. In those situations, you have to stand up for your team and be the person who accepts any consequences.

Takeaway: Strong leaders take bold actions when necessary and worry about the protocol later.

- Have you seen someone freeze and not act because they were not sure they had the authority to act? What were the consequences?

- Can you imagine a scenario in your role where you might need to act first and ask permission later?

LESSON 25

WEDDINGS, BABIES, HOSPITALS, AND FUNERALS

Weddings are optional, but funerals are mandatory. Be there for your people and they will be there for you. (Rudy Giuliani)

As a leader, your presence at team members' major life events means a tremendous amount. They admire you and most likely discuss you in some context to their families. When you make an appearance at a life event, it makes an impression. First, people are flattered that you would be at their event. Second, it elevates them in the eyes of people to whom they have spoken about you. Third, it helps build a bond of loyalty and trust with your team. Fourth, all the team members attending will realize the commitment of time you have made and will respect you for being generous with your time. Last, it will give you perspective of your team—their harmony and support for one another.

When your organization includes dozens, hundreds, or thousands of team members, it becomes impractical to participate in everyone's events. For your immediate staff, it is important to be as participative as possible. Attending their wedding, visiting a new baby, and stopping by to express concern when they are in the hospital or convalescing at home are things to try to do, if possible. But when the worst happens, you must be there.

If a member of your direct staff loses a close part of their family, you need to be there for them. They need your support and strength. They need to know that you understand their loss and grief. If you lose the team member on your staff, you have to step up for their family. They need someone strong to be there and help them deal with the situation. This is a critical part of being a leader: caring for your team as if part of your own family. Your immediate team is an extension of you.

When the loss is deeper down in the organization, it's very possible you had a very limited relationship with the team member. If so, you have to use your judgment: if your presence would actually be a distraction given that you were not close, you should pass on attending visitation or the service. On the other hand, there are many team members in the organization you may know very well and have worked with for years. Regardless of their position in the organization and yours, you should attend the services. You owe your colleague this respect, and it will mean a tremendous amount to the grieving members of the team.

These are poignant moments that demonstrate you are a member of the team, with feelings, dreams, and relationships just like them. It shows you care about the person as an individual, not just as a team member. Being there for life events, happy or sad, re-enforces your values.

EXAMPLE

An absolute tragedy occurred that cut short the life of one of our promising vice presidents. At the time, I was a manager who did not know the vice president, but I did have a lot of interaction with his boss, who was in charge of our division. The boss was a private man, someone who seemed cold, calculated, and quirky. He did not rise through the divisional ranks, so he did not have a history with the organization as a whole. To many, he was a boss that you could learn some from his strengths and a lot from his weaknesses as a leader. This event totally changed my perspective.

When the news circulated about the loss, the boss took charge. He was at the family's side immediately, and over the course of the next few weeks, he took wonderful care of the family. He arranged things to make the next couple of weeks as tolerable as possible for the family. He arranged things such as visitations for both the personal friends and family and then the workplace. He attended to all the funeral details. He worked behind the scenes with the human resources and benefits departments to simplify processes. Whatever the family needed for those weeks, he made sure it happened.

To many, this man's response was a shock. It challenged their perspective of him completely. You could see that he cared deeply for the people who worked for him. His actions demonstrated a human side few could see. Observing him in that time made an impression upon me. He demonstrated many of the qualities that I aspired to have. How he handled the situation was a lesson to all who thought of themselves as leaders.

Years later, I was home late on a Saturday night with a house full of teenagers who were playing Dance Dance Revolution when I got a call that one of my close colleagues, a friend, had unexpectedly found her spouse dead from natural causes at home. I didn't know who would be there with her, so at 11 p.m., I broke up the dance party and asked everyone to leave so that I could go be with her. I apologized to my daughter for ending her evening so abruptly and explained why I needed to go. When I arrived, to my relief, a few of my colleague's other close friends were with her. The police and medical personnel, perhaps the examiner, were all still there. We all stayed until matters were settled. The closest friends accompanied my colleague to the next location. Over the years, we looked back on that night, the conversations had and the situation in general, and were thankful we had that time together. It would have been easy to stay home that night and let the teenagers play until their curfew; it would have been easy to assume someone else would be there to comfort my friend. Live your values.

EXAMPLE

During the course of a long career, you will experience many life events. Sitting in on a baby shower at work for a beloved colleague was one of the more joyous and bizarre events I attended. It was bizarre in that I was playing baby shower games for the first time in my life (at a ripe old age of fifty-five) as a senior officer. Smell the diaper and guess the scent. Really? But the pending birth of my colleague's son was an important event and one that I had to celebrate.

Five years later, I attended a baby shower for my son and daughter-in-law (no smell the diaper games this time), and my daughter-in-law's boss, the CEO of her organization, was in attendance making a toast. On top of that, when my grandson was born the week of a board meeting, the CEO added a photo of the baby to her presentation, welcoming the newest member of the team! Imagine how my daughter-in-law felt about her boss; imagine how we, as the grandparents, felt about her boss! Those two simple gestures created life-long loyalty.

Similarly, there were times when we rallied at work to support a team member who had a tragedy beset them. The forum might be a prayer session or a potluck. Being there in the times of pain are as valuable, if not more so, than the times of joy. This is when we would see the family our organization had become. In addition, there were lots of visits to hospitals to check on my staff, regardless of whether it was they or their spouses, in the ICU or ER.

Unfortunately, the hardest times are when you lose a member of the team. The work family would be in pain but would rally together. The team member's manager would take charge. And as the senior leader, I would be there to support the family and the team as I could. This happened too many times and never got any easier. We lose too many in the prime of life. Funerals are mandatory.

Takeaway: Part of a leader's responsibility is to care for the whole welfare of their team. This includes personal events such as weddings, funerals, and births.

- Have you experienced a leader that has demonstrated their support by participating or attending such an event?
- How did others react to their involvement?

LESSON 26

DON'T BE AFRAID TO LEAD

There is nothing in the world as powerful as the single-minded pursuit of an idea.
(Frederick W. Smith)

When you see the opportunity or the need, lead. It might take some effort to get people to follow you, but that is what leadership is: getting people to rally together to achieve a common goal. So, if you feel strongly, do not be afraid to step up and lead.

Why do people hesitate and not lead? They are afraid to fail; instead, they should be afraid of not trying. They are afraid to risk something; as Nelson Mandela said, "courage was not the absence of fear, but the triumph over it." They don't believe in themselves. Most leaders have moments of doubt, but they know that to get people to follow them, they must project confidence. They think it's someone else's role; leaders see opportunities and seize them. If they wait for someone else, the opportunity might vanish.

In an interesting study of dynasty caliber championship sporting teams, author Sam Walker determined that leadership might contribute more to the long-term success of a team than other factors such as management, talent, and financial wherewithal. He theorizes that the leadership of one person who is giving his or her all can elevate the performance of the collective group. Through the leadership of a captain, a team can overcome obstacles and defeat more talented opponents.[16]

EXAMPLE

The Columbus, Ohio, sales market was a great potential market for FedEx. The city was a major distribution hub with dozens of large fulfillment centers, a nice manufacturing base, and a large number of retail industry headquarters and operations centers. The problem with the market was that just sixty-five miles down the road in Wilmington, Ohio, sat DHL's North American hub, and the UPS hub in Louisville was an hour closer than the FedEx hub in Memphis. Because of the better proximity of their hubs, UPS and DHL could let customers process shipments later into the night than FedEx could. The FedEx Express shipments had to leave Columbus nearly an hour earlier than DHL and thirty-five minutes earlier than UPS. Despite superior service, quality, and reliability, this made it difficult to compete for some accounts where they wanted the ability to ship until 10:30 p.m. or even 11:00 p.m. If FedEx could move their flight back or add a second flight that left later, there was tremendous revenue and market share to be gained.

That was the scenario I stepped into when I became the senior officer assigned to the Columbus market. For the market to grow Express volume, we needed flight time parity or superiority to the competition. That meant selling the idea of a later flight or a second flight to the engineering staff at our Memphis headquarters. The engineers who set the flight schedule were amazingly detailed people who maximized not only minutes but seconds in terms of getting planes in and out of the Memphis Hub each night. There were very specific reasons as to why flights from cities such as Columbus were scheduled when they were. So to change the schedule, there had to be a major reason to do it.

To win this battle, I enlisted the local sales team and had to get them to buy into a vision: if we got extra volume, we'd need a second plane. If we got a second flight out of Columbus, we could get a later flight time. With a later flight time, they could sell that to their customers to generate the extra volume. But they had to fill up the early plane with volume that was not as sensitive to pick-up times as other volume. That would help everyone: better service to customers, more revenue for the company, more sales for the team, more opportunity to make bonuses—and FedEx would take market share. They believed in the vision and were right behind me.

Soon I learned that I really needed them right beside me. When I first presented the vision to the engineering team in Memphis, we discussed what they would need to support us. The answer was a hard justification based on the volume and revenue to be gained. So I went back to the sales team and asked for detailed accounts where we could get the business and roughly what the revenue would be. Committing to the revenue numbers made people nervous. So we started making calls to target customers so I could gage the customer's enthusiasm firsthand. I was convinced we had a better value proposition and would win the business if we could guarantee the later flights. The sales manager believed as well. We quantified the opportunities and revenue potential.

I took it back to the engineers and pitched the concept: we could add millions in revenue with a new flight. We could dominate the market. The engineers had the costs of the new flight. Our revenues could justify the operational costs of the flight. But they wanted us to pay for the ownership costs of the plane as well. This was a first, as the company already had the plane on lease. They were not going out and adding a plane to the fleet to support this request. Basically, we were being told we had to justify the acquisition of a new jet aircraft, and that was no small number.

The sales manager and I still believed in the possibilities and that there was more opportunity to be found. We thought our team had been conservative. Again, we pitched the vision to the local sales team and implored them to believe, "build it, and they will come." As they saw our commitment to the effort and belief in the end result, they started to find more confidence. We documented three times more revenue potential.

Back to the engineers again. With my sales manager in tow, we pitched a new commitment amount. In effect, we would cover the total cost of the plane and operations through the additional revenue. The sales manager and I put our necks on the line. The debate in the room was ferocious. Then one executive spoke up, saying, "Folks, they are offering you all that revenue and putting their reputations on the line. You have made changes for a lot less before. Give them a chance." And we got the plane.

Unfortunately, it's hard to sometimes sell promises. Until the new flight was in service and customers could believe in it, volume was slow to ramp up. The engineers wanted to pull the flight. Then something that we did not anticipate happened. DHL, with their hub just down the road, announced they would be closing operations. Customers who valued shipping product as late as possible started looking for alternatives and found it: our second flight. It was the last one out of the market, and coupled with FedEx's great service and aggressive pricing, it was the answer to their needs. And since it filled our plane, it was the answer to my needs.

I'd like to think that our flight had a lot of impact on the success of FedEx in winning DHL customers. Truly, the company would have added flights immediately when DHL made its announcement. Our flight just gave us a head start. But that head start was because two of us believed, brought others along to see the vision, refused to accept *no*, sold the idea, and stayed committed until it worked. We put our reputations on the line. We were not afraid to lead.

Takeaway: When leaders are courageous in their convictions and giving it their all, people will follow.[17]

- Within your organization, when have you witnessed people rallying around someone who stepped up with passion?

- When have you stepped up and taken the lead on a new initiative or idea?

- With hindsight, what would you do the same or differently?

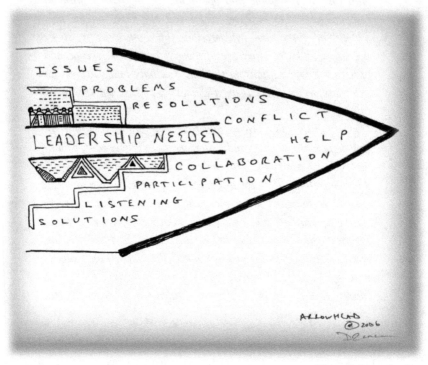

Figure 5: Arrowhead

LESSON 27

SPHERES OF INFLUENCE VS. CONTROL

God grant me the serenity to accept the things I cannot change, the courage to change the things I can, and the wisdom to know the difference. (The Serenity Prayer)

L eadership classes often teach about spheres of influence and control. There are things you can control, things you can influence, and then there is everything else (meaning what you cannot control). Leaders are taught a series of exercises to differentiate between the spheres.

The Serenity Prayer tells us to accept what we cannot change, have the courage to change what we can, and have the wisdom to know the difference. The key to the prayer may reside in "the courage to change the things I can." Leaders should change things for the better *when they can*. Sometimes it takes tremendous courage to do it. People who decided they could change things led the Civil Rights Movement. But it took tremendous courage for those leaders to face the hate and dangers hurled their way.

Maya Angelou has given us what is almost an addendum to the Serenity Prayer. She wrote the following:

You don't like something, change it.
If you can't change it, change your attitude.

Have the wisdom to know if you can change something. If so, possess the courage to change it. If you cannot change something, accept that, and manage your attitude.

There are times when we all bristle against something. We may burn huge amounts of energy worrying about it. We may burn significant amounts of time debating it. When it is not in our sphere of influence, we have wasted the time and energy.

EXAMPLE

After a series of corporate implosions, regulatory failures, and security breaches, a sweeping series of regulations were imposed on Corporate America. These included SOX404 compliance and credit card controls called PCI. To comply with those new regulations, major process changes and controls had to be implemented. To say that there was a lot of time spent debating and bristling against how the processes were being implemented would be an understatement. This was a time when we did not have a choice but to comply. In hindsight, this was one of many times when we needed to take the Serenity Prayer to heart and add Maya Angelou's point that we needed to change our attitude.

We need to help our teams delineate between what we can change and what we cannot. We need to help the teams manage attitude and focus. Most importantly, when we can change things for the better, we need to summon the courage to serve and lead.

Takeaway: As leaders, we need to be in tune with what is within our sphere of influence and what is not.

- How does this lesson apply to biblical leaders such as Jesus, Moses, and others? Historical figures like Gandhi, Martin Luther King, and the United States' Founding Fathers?

- What challenges do you see in the workplace and community?

- What do you need to do to have an impact and make change happen?

LESSON 28

BAD SURPRISES ARE A BAD IDEA

Don't wait to deliver bad news. No one wants a bad surprise. (David Zanca)

D o not wait to deliver bad news. It makes people question your integrity and begin to wonder why you would hesitate: are you asleep at the wheel? Are you cowardly? Is there a lack of basic institutional controls to make sure mistakes do not go unnoticed?

A good practice is to make sure you classify issues and risks and then communicate status based on the classification. For example, if a problem is not severe and can be mitigated, you probably will not escalate that to others. If a problem is serious, meaning that a project or operation will be impacted, and the duration of the impact is understood, you will want to make sure others know. If a catastrophic situation arises where a project or operation is impacted with no understood time to recover, you must communicate ASAP.

EXAMPLE

If we had an issue arise, our rule was to determine if it was something we could remedy before it turned serious or catastrophic or if it was too late. When the situation reached serious, we would share the news at the next appropriate instance; that might be a status report or the next project review. Should the

> *situation be catastrophic, regardless of the nature of the project, these occurrences need to be communicated ASAP. Waiting to try to get better information or an action plan was not a good strategy—the constituency needed to know that "Houston, we have a problem."*

When there is a problem, no one likes to be blind-sided by a third party delivering the news to the boss. Imagine when the boss learns of a problem from an unhappy customer rather than from his or her own team. Or worse yet, from the media! Avoid those situations, and proactively share bad news. Then the boss is prepared if and when the customer or the media calls.

This rule applies to your personal life as well. When loved ones get surprised by discovering news from someone other than you, the trust in the relationship is strained. Waiting until the last moment to deliver bad news is also a poor practice. Come clean as soon as you know there is a situation.

Takeaway: Who likes a bad surprise? When there is bad news, it's better to signal and share rather than wait and hope it goes away.

- Have you experienced a time at work or in your personal life when a bad surprise was revealed, and people reacted strongly? What could have been done instead?

- When in your role do you believe it would be ill advised to sit on bad news?

- When and how could you share bad news to avoid surprises?

LESSON 29

DELIVER EVEN IF YOU HAVE TO OVERRUN THE BUDGET

No one gets fired for overrunning a budget if they deliver; they get fired for not delivering.
(Andersen Consulting Partner)

C ustomers and constituents expect a supplier, vendor, or business partner to deliver to their expectations. If they do not, the consequences are ugly: you may face a money-back guarantee failure, a penalty or even a lawsuit, and the loss of the account or relationship. These consequences can be such that you or your group may face professional exposure. Project failures lead to discipline.

While customers and constituents detest failures, they are more tolerant of delays or project overruns as long as there is a degree of confidence that the end result will be achieved. There will be noise and emotion, penalties and pain, but delivering late or over budget is not as career threatening as failing to deliver.

In the consulting world, one common business arrangement is to work on a fixed fee basis. You estimate the effort and commit to a project cost before starting. If you can deliver the project for less than your estimate, you keep the difference. If you overrun the project, you eat the cost. This is a risky format from which to work. Often you discover that somehow the scope is a little different from what you understood it to be during estimation. Sometimes there are resource or technical issues. The list of risks is long.

EXAMPLE

When we were working under such an arrangement once, I shared with my boss a concern about a part of the project that we had not understood thoroughly and would need to add resources to cover. I suggested a few alternatives to minimize the cost overrun, but my boss instructed me to do whatever was needed to make sure we met the client's expectations. His rationale was simple: the consequences for not delivering to expectations is a lot worse than overrunning budget.

EXAMPLE

When my team at FedEx faced delays and overruns, we escalated the information as quickly as possible with a realistic revision of the plan. It is critical to make sure the customer or constituent understands that the objective of the project can still be achieved. They will not be happy with the bad news, but as long as the revised plans are realistic and get to the end state, they will be more accepting. Of course, there are a few exceptions where the deadline is a "true drop dead" (Y2K remediation for IT is an example) or where you cannot get the resources or funds to complete an overrun. But those are exceptions.

Takeaway: Your role as a leader is to motivate a group to accomplish a goal. Achieving the goal must be a priority. Therefore it is important that you do not accept failure unless unavoidable. Develop mitigating actions and plans to achieve the goal even if it overruns a budget or schedule.

- If you need to reset a project plan or adjust a schedule due to an issue, how would you frame the news?

- Have you seen projects that went over budget or over schedule but were still considered a success when delivered? If so, what did the project leadership do to retain credibility? How did they make it feel successful?

LESSON 30

WHEN FACED WITH SETBACKS AND CRITICISMS, KEEP PERSPECTIVE

Haters gonna hate, hate, hate. . . . Shake it off, shake it off. (Taylor Swift)

T here will be times when you as a leader are criticized. You may have some setbacks. This will happen. When it does, you have to work hard to keep it in perspective. A servant leader will often take setbacks or criticisms personally, as they really want to do right and serve others.

Using techniques to depersonalize the situation is important. Remember the concept of spheres of influence versus control (lesson 27). There are some things you can control, some you can influence, and some that you have no control over. Determine which situation you face. If it's out of your control, you have to let go and not let it nag at you. If you control it, work with your team, boss, or mentor to develop an action plan. If you can influence it, you have to develop a strategy.

EXAMPLE

When an issue impacted company operations, and my group was the root cause, I took it personally, feeling like

I personally let the company down. I was accountable for our organization, and that sense of responsibility was appropriate. But that is different from being personally responsible. Personalizing the team's mistakes eats at you. Being able to compartmentalize situations is a valuable technique and lets you separate personal from organizational responsibilities.

At other times, we would face criticisms for different issues. I learned early that you cannot listen to all the critics. Fortunately, a business partner of mine told me that if some people were not complaining, I would not be doing my job. He went on to say that if everyone was complaining, then we might have a problem. So our group developed a listening post that could measure the intensity of concerns and whether we needed to act. For example, we would monitor customer feedback on product changes. When we would receive extremely negative feedback, we could test it in our listening post to see if there were similar complaints or if there were any positive comments on the same changes. That could tell us if the criticism was a real issue or not.

There are times when your confidence may get shaken. You will start to believe that the impostor police are coming to your door. These are the times when you have to have deep fortitude and know the mirror technique. You have to be able to look at yourself in the mirror and ask, *Am I doing everything I can to make my teams successful? Am I doing right for them and for the company?* If you can answer yes, it's time to channel Taylor Swift and "shake it off."

Takeaway: All leaders face criticism. You will not make everyone happy all the time. Develop mechanisms to avoid taking criticism personally. Also, develop mechanisms to determine what criticism is valid and needs addressing.

- When faced with criticism, is it of a political, personal, or irrational nature? If so, should you invest energy worrying about it?

- Identify a leader you admire, and ask them how they handle criticism. How do they avoid letting it become personal?

CHAPTER THREE:

MANAGERIAL LESSONS

THREE: INTRODUCTION

Recall the distinction that Peter Drucker made regarding leadership and management: "Management is doing things right. Leadership is about doing the right things." I draw a slightly different distinction between a manager and a leader. Some leaders are managers; some leaders are not. All managers should be leaders; but some are not. This chapter contains a series of lessons valuable to someone in a managerial role. The lessons in this chapter are intended for the person who is in management and is or aspires to be a leader.

As before, the beneficiary of these lessons is intended to be at all levels of the management ladder. Anyone managing a team should be able to apply these learnings to their situation. The responsibilities of each level of management may vary, but the principles of treating people well, encouraging a team, recognizing achievement, and creating a safe, fun work environment applies to all.

Over my thirty-two years in business, twenty-eight were spent managing team members. My assignments placed me in eleven different management roles, ranging from frontline manager through middle and to senior management. In the consulting world, the frontline manager directs resources assigned to their project and provides performance evaluations based on that project. Formal career planning and salary administration is conducted at a centralized level. In the corporate world, my discovery was that as a frontline manager, I was responsible for daily performance, career planning, salary administration, and just about every other attribute of my team members' experience. As I progressed, I was directly managing other managers and a small number of staff while leading the organization as a whole. During that journey, I found that each of these corporate management positions had a few common responsibilities, while each was different from the other. The teams each had a unique personality, the challenges were different, and the pressures from the superiors were different. The common ground was talent recognition, performance management, team building, and creating an environment where everyone was safe and comfortable so they could work hard.

At the same time, Ginny and I were rearing two wonderful children. Our daughter was gregarious, creative, and sensitive. Our son was quieter, athletically inclined, and kind. As with most siblings, they had different personalities, and each needed a little different parenting style. This was true as a manager as well. Our team members had differing personalities and motivations. You had to manage each slightly differently.

As a parent, you care deeply about the well-being of your children. Similarly, as a manager, I cared about the well-being of my team members. That meant getting to know them, their family situation, and their dreams and aspirations. Once you were committed to the team members, they could commit to you.

In parenting, we would hold our children to high standards of behavior. As a manager, I would expect the same of my team members. As parents, we would try to re-enforce behaviors and encourage our children. This applied to my teams at work. Celebration of birthdays or other milestones was another lesson I carried over from parenthood to management. I am not suggesting that every lesson in this chapter applies to both parenting and management, but there are certainly similarities.

LESSON 31

THE TOUGHEST JOB IS ON THE FRONT LINE

The problem for managers is that they have to take responsibility for their part in the organization, but they have to do so in a context that they can never completely control. (Paul Corrigan)[18]

E veryone in an organization is challenged in one way or another: maybe the challenges are in creating a vision, setting the direction to achieve the vision, building the tactical plans to win, and executing against the plan. But those frontline people, whether delivering service to the customer or executing the plan, are the ones with some of the greatest challenges. They are tasked with delivering and have multiple pressures working on them. Granted, executive and senior management have incredible pressures and lots of conflicting constituencies, but they also have a lot more resources available to manage those pressures. For those on the front line, it's often *mano e' mano* (as in hand-to-hand combat).

For the frontline manager, they have the assignment to deliver on their objective while caring for the welfare of their team and implementing policy from above, which at times can be controversial at the team member level. They have to make things happen with the resources they have, keep the team together, drive change, and support the vision or policies of the company. It's a tough balancing act.

Senior and executive management needs to think about how they support the front line with the best communications possible, regarding vision, purpose, and mission. When policy changes come, empower the front line with great materials and support from above. Sometimes, an effective technique is for upper management to meet directly with the frontline management. This provides an opportunity for the frontline managers to ask questions, voice concerns, and then hear responses directly from upper levels in an unfiltered manner. Use surveys of team members to gather information and measure attitudes, but don't use it as a weapon to beat up managers.

EXAMPLE

There are few entry-level management positions with more responsibility than the platoon leader in the military. Accomplishing the mission is job one, but they are also tasked with caring for the welfare of their troops. They are responsible for them in virtually all aspects of their life: in personal matters, health, training, career, and when on missions. The role is 24/7, and the people doing it are doing it for the first time in their careers.

When deployed on a mission and complications arise, you have to improvise with the resources you have. The platoon leader can ask for help, but it's typically not just down the hall. The role of platoon leader may be the extreme example of the toughest frontline manager job. The corporate manager's job is difficult but not as dangerous and the consequences not quite as severe. Real rounds are not usually landing around the corporate manager. Nevertheless, the frontline corporate manager job is difficult.

EXAMPLE

Interestingly, my daughter experienced a similar challenge as a frontline manager at Disney. After graduating from college, she joined the team at Disney World and was quickly promoted into management in food and beverage services. Soon she was the shift manager at their premier restaurant in the Magic Kingdom. Much like a young platoon leader, she was charged with tremendous responsibility while having limited experience. She would be responsible for twenty or thirty employees per shift— many of whom were international workers from places such as China, Haiti, the Philippines, and Jamaica. In addition to her responsibilities to ensure customer satisfaction, comply with all health and sanitation regulations, complete accounting and HR processes, and work with a unionized workforce, she also had culture clashes between employees, language difficulties, customer issues, and changing corporate mandates to manage.

EXAMPLE

We expected our managers to handle the challenges described above while meeting deadlines and delivering with quality. At the same time, they were always being asked ad hoc questions (fire drills, really). They had to make sure that all processes and procedures were being followed; they had to make sure all controls were being implemented. Then we started to add the complications: we would change the scope of their project but not the due date, pull a resource, add additional controls and procedures, and assign them or their team members to task forces.

As if that was not enough, we'd introduce major changes that they would have to sell to their teams. For example, the senior team decided to use offshore resources instead of local contract resources to supplement our workforce. The managers would lose line-of-sight management abilities with six thousand miles and fourteen hours of time difference between them and the offshore resources. The team was resistant to the idea in the beginning. The manager had to sell them on the long-term benefits of the change even though everyone knew there would be short-term pain. Meanwhile, the manager would need to deal with all the personnel related matters such as motivating, encouraging, growing, and leading a team.

Takeaway: Middle to senior management needs to remember how difficult a job the frontline manager has. Empowering them with information and providing as much flexibility as possible can help them with tough situations and support change initiatives.

- What can you do to help the frontline manager?
- Are there good examples in your organization of leadership that does a great job supporting the front line?

LESSON 32

SEND PEOPLE TO "BE NICE SCHOOL"

Don't leave a meeting without the people in the meeting feeling good about themselves.
(Cathryn W. Pugh)

There are times when you have to give a leader coaching on how to treat people. Part of that coaching may be conversational, and part may require that you ask them to step aside and get help. Euphemistically, that help can be called "be nice school."

Sometimes you may work with a person in a position of authority who has little patience with team members who do not grasp concepts, see the big picture, or capture the details as quickly as that leader would like. The leader often treats these people as if they were slow, lazy, or foolish. Hence the expression that someone "doesn't suffer fools gladly." In such cases, the leader may be rude to a particular team member. The leader may work around the person and exclude them from activities and tasks.

In a life or death situation, this may be very appropriate behavior. There can be no tolerance for foolishness in combat. Other environments, such as volunteer organizations and the business world, are a little different. High-performance-based organizations quickly identify underachievers and counsel them, often to the point of a career change. Benevolent organizations that espouse values of respect, development, and growth approach this in a different manner. If the team member in question is making every effort to understand and contribute, they are not perceived as fools but rather as potential contributors who need more coaching, assistance, training, or other help. Of course, the benevolent organization also must make sure everyone is contributing appropriately, and if those steps fail to make the team member productive, a career change may be required.

For the leader in an organization that culturally respects people, they must learn to practice more patience. Not everyone is as quick or experienced as they. A strong leader seeks ways to maximize the resources on hand, and they try to simplify tasks and messages so all understand. If not, they leave team members behind. People left behind become disillusioned and disengaged.

At other times, leaders may frustrate talented and experienced team members because the leader does not listen to them or seek input. They may brush a team member's idea aside or ignore them completely. In this inverted case, the experienced team member may view the leader as slow, lazy, or arrogant. As in the scenario described above, this too can lead to resentment and disengagement of the team member.

To mitigate this, in people-oriented and team-based cultures, leaders have to be coached to avoid the "doesn't suffer fools gladly" idiom. Leaders have to respect their team members, help them along, and when it is not possible to continue, deal with the situation with grace and respect. Similarly, when team members get frustrated that their leaders do not listen or seek input, leaders need to face the criticism head on and change behavior.

EXAMPLE

In our workgroup at FedEx, we had an extraordinary individual who was a former college instructor and technical guru and had an extremely strong personality. She could go deep on areas of her expertise and bury you in the process. When you really needed to know how something worked or needed a solution to a problem, you turned to her. She was brilliant, articulate, and dedicated to our mission. She also did not "suffer fools gladly." When she would meet with other groups and explain how integration should work, she overpowered the room. People may have been intimidated by the strength of her personality or the depth she might go when presenting. They certainly were offended when she acted astounded at their basic questions. In the FedEx culture, that was not acceptable. As a result, our management would get complaints from the other groups requesting her to be reassigned. Our answer was, "No, we'll coach her." Reassignment would not address the issue. We had to change the behavior.

When the management team coached her, they explained the nature of the culture and that you have to have patience. The advice was typically, "slow down, simplify your message and language, and treat everyone with respect." Additionally, one of my advisors gave our brilliant technical leader some sage advice: "Don't leave a meeting without the people in the meeting feeling good about themselves." My advisor had learned this over the years because she too was a driver who could be demanding and thus rub people the wrong way. She learned this technique as a way to put velvet on her hammer. This advice was based on similar experiences and personalities, it reflected the culture, and it was very effective.

There were times I had management team members who did not listen to their teams, business partners, or peers and treated them poorly. They did not "suffer fools gladly." When I would tell them that we had time and resources to work with people who did not get it on the first try and that culturally it was important to keep our team, partners, and peers engaged, I'd get pushback. They felt I was asking them to accept low performance, laziness, or stupidity. That was not what I was asking. What I was asking was for them to be patient and work harder to get everyone to be productive, and if certain team members were not trying or capable, we would deal with that separately. The goal was to get our message across, meet our objective, not compromise quality, and develop our team in the process. If they did not know how to do this, I would send them to a figurative "be nice school."

After a few years of coaching leaders and managers in our organization to have some tolerance, this conversation about not "suffering fools gladly" became known as "be nice school." Everyone got the point that we were going to treat others with respect as long as people were engaged and trying.

Takeaway: You cannot tolerate behavior contrary to your organization's culture and values. If a leader behaves in such a way, you have to address it.

- Are there leaders you know who have been or need to be sent to "be nice school"?
- Was the coaching effective?
- What advice would you give to someone who is acting contrary to culture?

LESSON 33

HIRE TO YOUR WEAKNESSES

Never hire or promote in your own image. It is foolish to replicate your strength and idiotic to replicate your weakness. It is essential to employ, trust, and reward those whose perspective, ability, and judgment are radically different from yours. It is also rare, for it requires uncommon humility, tolerance, and wisdom. (Dee Hock)

In baseball, there are the few true superstars who can do it all: run, hit, hit with power, field, and throw. But ninety-nine percent of players do just a few of those things extremely well. This is also true in management. Few of us are great at everything. Some are visionary, and some are implementers. Some are direct, while others avoid conflict. Whatever your strengths, identify your weaknesses, and when you can, hire to address those gaps.

An additional benefit from hiring to your weaknesses is making sure you don't double stack leadership personality types. Building an organization with two or three successive layers of like dominate personality traits can stagnate an organization. For example, the Promoter—Analytic—Controller—Supporter model from Senn-Delaney identifies dominant personality types.[19] A supporter leading a supporter often leaves an organization with confused messaging and direction. A promoter leading a promoter results in a spectacular set of visions often difficult to achieve and with little execution focus. Analytical leading analytical can result in an organization that is process oriented: operationally excellent but limited in vision and support. Controller on top of controller type leads to a sub culture of micro management and concentrated decision making.

EXAMPLE

For years, I watched a visionary leader who could inspire the enterprise and describe the next big thing. What he did so wisely was surround himself with detail-oriented implementers who could take that vision, pare it down to an achievable reality, and make it happen. He hired to his weakness.

While working with the board of directors at two companies, I observed that well-planned boards are architected with differing skills and perspectives. Board members are carefully chosen to complement one another and ensure that the board has a range of skills.

Through observation in the workplace and at the board level, plus my own experiences, I learned and tried to architect teams. In my case, I was analytical and big picture oriented. Thus my team needed someone who would work the details and drive teams with a velvet hammer. The combination of seeing the big picture with a partner who could organize and drive made us a successful team. I know that partner made me a better leader and manager.

When I inherited work groups with analytical types working for me, we tended to overthink the process and execution details. Our ability to communicate, sell, and promote our solutions was missing. And our job was to push big culture changes through a massive six-thousand-person workforce! We needed balance in our styles to be successful. Be careful of double stacking personality types; you might overdose on common strengths.

Takeaway: Assess your talents. Strengthen your team by hiring to your weaknesses.

- What do you need on your team to complement your strengths?

- What gap in skills do you have that you need to hire in order to fill?

LESSON 34

DON'T PIGEONHOLE PEOPLE

Never tell someone what they can't accomplish. (Robert B. Carter)

For a manager, it's easy to fall into a familiar trap regarding team members and their roles. Sometimes you work with a person for a period of time and can only see them in that role. You have formed an impression that the person is capable of functioning at a certain level, but you don't have the ability to envision them serving in a different role. Then your team member or colleague comes forth and surprises you by volunteering to take on a new role, offering to step up to a particular challenge, or even inquiring about going into management. Your mental model of that person and their abilities has been completely bounded by the role in which they have served. Now you are challenged to imagine them doing something you never thought they would. Don't make the pigeonhole mistake. Be open-minded about the possibilities while being honest about the potential issues or barriers. Be positive in helping people evaluate their options and objective in deciding if they can succeed.

EXAMPLE

This mistake has slowed and hindered many a career of really good team members. One example is the solid team member who has served in a subject matter expert (SME) role for years and has been pigeonholed as a one trick pony. As the group SME, they are highly valuable for the depth of their knowledge in one area but are perceived to be of limited potential beyond that role. When a leadership role comes open, they are excluded from consideration. Why? Because they have allowed management to build a one-sided impression of their capabilities? Or is it because management isn't always open to the possibilities of someone growing and morphing right before their eyes?

Perhaps it is both. The team member must take the personal responsibility to grow and demonstrate that growth to management. But, more importantly, it's management's responsibility to look for the upside and potential in its team members and suspend disbelief. This doesn't mean management should blindly promote the team member; rather, it means they should encourage and fairly assess the possibilities instead of sending the team member back to the pigeon coop without a chance.

This is a mistake I made a few times in my management career. Good people who mastered their area over a course of eight to ten or more years would express interest in greater responsibilities. I had pigeonholed them in that area, perhaps thinking the longevity of their tenure was a lack of ambition or a flaw. Regardless of the reason, I was wrong. If I didn't support them, they would move on to other organizations and then demonstrate their abilities. After a few times, I realized my mistake and determined not to pigeonhole people. Instead, I would support people looking to improve themselves and not stand in their way.

Takeaway: People will surprise you when they are motivated and energized. Do not underestimate the power of someone's ambition.

- Have you seen people be pigeonholed? If so, why?
- Ever witnessed someone's ambition and spirit be crushed because they were told they could not achieve a goal?
- Is there anyone in your organization you should encourage to follow his or her ambitions?

LESSON 35

WALK THE HALLS— BE ACCESSIBLE

If you want engaged professionals, engage and listen to them—else you'll have day labor. (Anonymous)

T he people who are working hard in the trenches want to know they aren't being forgotten or taken for granted. They know best as to how their specific operation works and if there are opportunities for improvement. But, perhaps most importantly, they can give you true, unfiltered input regarding what is right and wrong in the organization, whether something is working or behind schedule. That is why David Packard of Hewlett-Packard fame first practiced what he referred to as "management by walking around."

EXAMPLE

Whenever our CEO happened to visit an operational group, he would go out of his way to walk the halls, shake hands, and chat with people. Of course, in this instance, he had rock star status, so that momentary brush with the CEO had a magnified impact on the team members. I contrast that with another rock star CEO with whom we engaged at their facilities and how he did virtually the opposite. He chose not to engage with his troops at all. It was very demoralizing for the team members. Similarly, while I was early in my career in the consulting field, the partners who took the time to swing by the workrooms and visit the consulting staff— ever so briefly—were the ones you wanted to work for and emulate.

Given these experiences, I always made an effort to be accessible, walk the halls, and chat with our team. If we had a particularly hard change occurring or a complicated project, I'd spend more time probing and listening. What I discovered was that information through the management chain was often filtered. The information was true but sometimes only half true. These hallway chats and coffee pot visits gave our team members a feeling that we lived our values and sought truth.

There are other ways to accomplish this. For example, eating lunch in the cafeteria makes you visible and accessible. If your team is in a locale across town that you can only visit occasionally, schedule coffee, breakfast, or lunch with a small group of the team members at a more convenient location. Find ways to get firsthand feedback and build rapport with your team members. Occasionally, schedule "walk" time on your calendar to make sure you do it.

Takeaway: Your team knows you are busy, but they also want to know they matter. Make time to be accessible.

- How do you proactively ensure that you are accessible?
- Schedule times, appointments, lunches, or coffee meetings to be available.
- What do you do with the feedback you receive from the team?

LESSON 36

FIND A TIME FOR HUMOR AND HAVE SOME FUN

Today, we are not just spending a day at the beach . . . we are all participating in mandatory fun activities. Funtivities! And there is a special secret prize for the winner! (Michael Scott, "The Office")

There is a reason that *work* is a four-letter word. It can be hard, frustrating, rewarding, and motivating, but rarely is it inherently *fun*. And we know the old adage, "all work and no play . . ." So it is important to carve out some time and find ways to add some fun to the workplace. There are hundreds of possibilities, but don't make it just another task for your team. You have to make these things fun to participate in and something they want to do. So let them design and organize most of it. Of course, Halloween, Christmas, and springtime all lend themselves to activities.

EXAMPLE

One thing people enjoy is when the leadership makes fun of themselves and cuts up in appropriate fashion at these activities. Sometimes it would be dressing up in costume and performing. Twenty years later, people at our company spoke of two executives dressing up as the Blues Brothers and performing at a national sales rally. In our group, we had a tradition of celebrating Christmas with our leadership, writing and performing a satirical Christmas themed skit every year. One year it was funny Christmas cards; another year it was mock gifts for certain people; another year it was changing the lyrics to Christmas carols. People looked forward to the Christmas roast and seeing the lighter side of the leadership team.

EXAMPLE

Another fun thing I tried to do for the management team was to personally host a special holiday party. The first few years, we bought tickets to a local theater Christmas play for the team and their dates, spouses, or partners. At the theater I'd host a wine and cheese party before and after the show. This worked great for a few years when the shows were lighthearted Christmas shows such as "Tuna Christmas" and the "Sanders Family Christmas Show." Even David Sedaris's "Santaland Diaries" was a success.

The last year I did this (spoiler alert—last year) the local theater produced a new play, "The Reindeer Monologues." So my wife and I booked the party room and bought a block of eighty tickets. We invited my management team as in years past and this particular year included key business partners and their dates, spouses, and partners. The show had a reputation of being dark, but I figured it would work out like the "Santaland Diaries" did with an upbeat ending. Don't all Christmas shows end happily?

We all enjoyed a great pre-show reception and then headed in for the show. From the first moments of the show, I knew this was a mistake. The show was darker than dark. I could only imagine how I was ruining Christmas for everyone. There were a couple of laughs, but the show just got darker and darker. And when the house lights came up, I prayed that it wasn't for an intermission! This show had found a way to offend everyone. Fortunately, it was over, and my wife and I went into damage control mode. We were apologizing to everyone. As soon as I got home, I sent everyone an email with my apologies. Most people laughed it off, admitting that they probably wouldn't have gone to the show on their own. A few loved the avant-garde nature of the show. And over time, the evening grew in legend. It gave people something to always tease me about—including the reindeer sweatshirts and antlers at my retirement party.

Takeaway: Fortunately, there is time in most professions for a little levity and fun. Finding the time and place is important for team morale.

- What does your organization do to create some fun and encourage teamwork?

- How can you set an example for your team? What activities might lighten the workday?

- Do you have team members who are creative and would enjoy working on this?

Figure 6: Faux Christmas Card (1)

Figure 7: Faux Christmas Card (2)

Figure 8: Faux Christmas Card (3)

Figure 9: Faux Christmas Card (4)

Figure 10: Faux Christmas Card (4)

Figure 11: Team Building

LESSON 37

CHEER PROGRESS AND CELEBRATE VICTORIES

We treat our people like royalty. If you honor and serve the people who work for you, they will honor and serve you. (Mary Kay Ash)

Great leaders know that the journey to achieving most goals is difficult. You must navigate the risks you anticipated and the risks you could have never anticipated, the complications, personnel matters, and good and bad luck. That is why great leaders don't wait to the end before cheering their team. If you wait too long, it might not work out as you planned. Jump in during the journey and cheer your team members by recognizing and honoring their sacrifice and commitment, celebrating small victories along the way. Positive feedback during the process helps the team reconnect to the importance of the mission and their specific contributions. It gives them encouragement to push forward.

When you do arrive at the destination, celebrate! Leaders recognize the hard work and results, even when there are some things left undone or needing correction. Celebrate the victory as a way to say thank you to the team member and for re-enforcement of the goal achieved. Do not dwell on tasks left to accomplish, and there usually are some, but instead on the achievement and how it fits into the larger picture of the organization as a whole.

EXAMPLE

Entrepreneurs offer a great case study of leaders who understand that they need to celebrate the small victories and cheer the team forward on their journey. They understand the rollercoaster ride of a start-up and know that for every peak there will be a valley. Because it requires a lot of energy to make a climb, celebrating each peak is important. It gives the team satisfaction and a sense of accomplishment, even though everyone knows there will still be hard days ahead. Cheering and celebrating along the journey creates good will for the rest of the ride.

EXAMPLE

In the corporate world, the product development lifecycle can span years. The lifecycle may span concept, definition, financial and operational feasibility, market assessments, production build out and sourcing, and finally a product launch. If you wait until launch to cheer or celebrate, you missed the opportune time to connect with your team. They need some recognition at milestones along the journey. When the going gets tough, they need positive words of encouragement. During the longest days of the effort, when the team begins to feel they have been sentenced to hard labor, they need a break and a shot of enthusiasm.

Our team went through one of these projects. We celebrated milestones and recognized individuals for their extraordinary hard work as the project progressed. We tried to break the grind by mixing up surprises and treats—such as fresh fruit baskets for a month, a surprise ice cream sundae break, and even a movie break in the auditorium. When we got to the minimal viable product, we had a big celebration. The product was not complete; we all knew that, and we knew the minimal viable product had a lot of issues with it. But it was a huge step forward.

Others in the corporation did not understand why we would stop at that point and celebrate because the product was nowhere near where it needed to be to capture the market. What they did not know was how hard the journey to that stage was and how much our team members invested to get to this point. This was symbolically the right milestone to celebrate in a big fashion: we were going to market! The base product now existed, and there was no longer any doubt that we would get to the full product set and win in the marketplace.

To apply a sports analogy, a sporting event or game would be pretty boring to a spectator if you could not cheer during the game. The players would not get that little extra boost of adrenaline from the crowd. Waiting to the end deprives everyone the joy and satisfaction of celebrating good efforts along the way. Cheering and encouraging throughout the game is an important tool in the coach's toolbox. While it doesn't make sense to give out trophies at halftime, it does make sense to recognize outstanding effort and encourage the right behaviors.

Takeaway: Keep encouraging your team throughout a long project or journey. Take moments along the way to say "thanks" and "job well done." When you get to the end, celebrate!

- Is *cheering* an acceptable practice in your organization and role? Or is your organization a *celebration only* culture?
- How can you keep your teams motivated and valued in a long, hard effort?
- What ways can you cheer the team?
- Could you apply this to your personal life?

LESSON 38

MEASURE EFFORT AND KNOW HOW HARD PEOPLE WORK

You can only manage what you measure. (W. Edwards Deming)

O ur team members never failed to amaze with their dedication and work ethic. In a high stress 24/7 environment with pending deadlines, our folks were professionals who cared deeply about the quality and delivery of our mission. They would work long hours, weekends, and holidays as needed, often to the detriment of family or personal life. It was not a sweatshop environment but one where the pride and love for the mission combined with individual work ethic resulted in their tremendous commitment. The fear you should have in circumstances such as this is *burnout*. Personal lives can unravel, or team members can hit the stress wall. The consequences are devastating. Certainly, adequate workload, staffing, and project planning is necessary to avoid the sweatshop, but still, pressures remain. Monitor the team and look for signs of overload.

EXAMPLE

Because of the stress of deadlines and complexity of our work, our staff put in long hours, compounded by the necessity to be on call every night. To understand the wear and tear on the team, we analyzed time system data to monitor who was consistently working forty-five hours or more every week. When we would see individuals putting in fifty, sixty, and sometimes even more hours repeatedly, it would call for investigation. Was the workload unreasonable? Were the deadlines too tight? Were there quality issues that needed addressing? Was the individual someone who just loved the job and gladly put in the time? Sometimes there were actionable items to improve quality of life. By measuring, monitoring, and acknowledging to the team member that we as a management team knew how hard they were working, the individual knew someone cared and was appreciative.

Takeaway: Strong leaders know the strain and effort their team is under.

- Do you have a way to measure effort and stress?
- Can you take action to improve the burden on team members?
- Do they know you know how hard they are working?
- How can you apply this to your personal life?

Figure 12: Food Truck Rodeo

LESSON 39

USE FAILURES AS A TEACHING OPPORTUNITY

Failure is a lesson learned, success is a lesson applied. (Anonymous)

The child stands—holding on—then lets go and stands independently, albeit wobbly. Next there is the attempt for a first step, and down he or she goes. The process is repeated until balance and movement are mastered. Failure, repeated a few times, has taught another child how to walk. This pattern will repeat itself hundreds of times in his or her life: tying a shoe, riding a bike, missing a shot. Parents and educators view failures or setbacks as learning moments. They re-enforce the good, correct the negative, and encourage for the future. Leaders in business should as well.

When there is a systemic failure, it is the perfect opportunity to use it as a teaching moment. By the definition, the failure is not something isolated to an individual or a single area. The failure occurs at a higher, larger level. No one entity is to be reprimanded, but the whole needs remediation to avoid future occurrences. This is a wonderful teaching opportunity.

When a failure occurs at the individual or work group level, coaching is a valuable tool to draw lessons from the failure, put the incident into perspective, and find motivation to try again. This does not mean there isn't a consequence to the failure; a good manager can separate consequences from the coaching.

EXAMPLE

Shortly after I rotated into one of my new assignments, we were well behind on a major integration project, and I needed to brief executive management on the consequences and root causes. When we started to dig into the root causes, the findings grabbed my attention. The project was almost doomed from the start. The team worked hard but had no chance, and worse yet, they did not speak up. They just plugged along because their prior management did not tolerant bad news. This was an opportunity to establish our values and improve our processes.

In 2006 consulting company VitalSmarts worked with The Concours Group to produce a seminal study on why large projects failed. We found that the root causes identified in the study were very consistent with our situation. The study was "Silence Fails," and it highlighted five core issues that cause project failure.[20] Four of the five fit to our situation and were great training on how we wanted to avoid this for the future. No one was reprimanded; no one was punished; this was an opportunity for us to learn and grow. Years later that team continued to use the program to emphasize the points. The lesson was successful.

Takeaway: Experience is a powerful teacher. Unfortunately, most the lessons learned from experience seem to be painful. Failure has proven to be one of the greatest teachers.

- Think of a time you made a major mistake or experienced a failure. What did you learn from each?

- Have you been able to apply learnings from your mistakes to future situations and avoid the same result?

- How would you counsel a team member who has experienced a failure or setback?

LESSON 40

DON'T LET THE URGENT GET IN THE WAY OF THE IMPORTANT

Most of us spend too much time on what is urgent and not enough time on what is important. (Stephen Covey)

In 1954 President Dwight D. Eisenhower made famous the concept of the urgent and the important in what would be known as the "Eisenhower Principle." If there is anyone who understands the difference between urgent and important, it is probably a former five-star general, supreme commander of allied troops in World War II, and president of the United States. Those are pretty good credentials!

Steven Covey, in *The Seven Habits of Highly Effective People* further popularized the Eisenhower Principle. Covey explains the principle and provides a tool to help people classify activities in one of four quadrants:

1. Important and Urgent (such as going to the doctor when sick, meeting a tax deadline);

2. Important but Not Urgent (refining a vision, doing research on future trends, investing in developmental time);

3. Not Important but Urgent (answering the phone, responding to emails the moment you receive them); and

4. Not Important and Not Urgent (reading social media posts, playing video games).

What is important and what is urgent? *Important* activities shape our ability to achieve goals and define the future. *Urgent* activities require immediate attention and typically involve other people's goals. We tend to respond to the urgent to avoid the consequences of not responding. But, in doing so, it interferes with the important.[21]

Our lives, both professionally and privately, are faced with the Eisenhower Principle. We have to choose where to invest our time and energy. The key is to concentrate energy on the *important* items, while giving appropriate time to the *urgent but not important* activities and not letting those priorities flip-flop.

EXAMPLE

A great example in the business world is allowing email to consume your time to the detriment of leading your team. Many emails are urgent and important and do require timely attention. But most are either not important and not urgent (items where you are copied, informational) or urgent and not important (requests from others for information, input, reviews).

My mentor walked into my office one day and found me working away on email. He looked over my shoulder and said, "Get out of that thing. There is very little important stuff in there. We need you out creating energy and making things happen." He was right. My having a priority of keeping a clean inbox or being the first to respond to a request was far from the best use of my time.

That is one simple example; there are many more. It is very easy to get sucked into the rabbit hole of chasing *urgent* items and not getting to the true *important* leadership tasks. And in your private life, it is just as easy. You can get caught up in the book club, the softball team, or the reality show and not attend to the *important* activities that you need to realize your dreams. Check your priorities and see if you are guilty of placing the *urgent* ahead of the *important*. I was.

Takeaway: Use your time and energy wisely. Focus on the important.

- Which of your events or activities are urgent but not important?

- How can you differentiate between the urgent and important?

- Do you have role models that manage the urgent/important well?

LESSON 41

WHEN MAKING TOUGH DECISIONS, SEEK INPUT, BUT NOT EVERYTHING IS DECIDED BY CONSENSUS

Use the formula P = 40 to 70, in which P stands for the probability of success and the numbers indicate the percentage of information acquired . . . Once the information is in the 40 to 70 range, go with your gut. (General Colin Powell)

As we have already established, leaders don't have all the answers. If you don't have the answers, some decisions will be tough. For those, you will want information as input. You will want input from valued colleagues. But rarely will you ever get all the information to make the decision easy, nor will you get feedback from all your colleagues. You will have to make decisions with imperfect information. Especially in situations when there is a time constraint or an impeding emergency, gathering all the information or building a consensus is not effective.

"Heavy is the head that wears the crown," wrote William Shakespeare. This is true for you also. If you are in charge, ultimately, you have to make the decision. You can ask for information. You can seek input. The responsibility and accountability rests with you.

There are a few times when consensus matters, but for the tough, time sensitive decisions, the leader has to make the call. Do not abdicate the responsibility.

An old adage related to this is, "The best leaders get ninety percent of the decisions right with only fifty percent of the information being available." General Colin Powell famously reframed the concept in his "P = 40 to 70" formula. The common piece between the two is that you have to make a decision with less than perfect information, and that means going with your gut—not consensus. Intuition is a very powerful tool for a leader.

EXAMPLE

In an organization with a leader, is groupthink an appropriate form of decision making, and do people really buy in and commit to a consensus decision? At the end of the day, who is accountable for the decision? A group of people or the leader? In a hierarchal type structure, consensus might work for deciding where to go to lunch, but for the hard decisions, the leader needs to gain input and then decide. There is a critical addendum to the decision-making process: once the decision is made, the leader must ensure that everyone is aligned and committed to making the decision successful.

I always sought input into major decisions. There were certain trusted voices to whom I would turn. We would bounce alternatives around and debate the consequences. Then a decision would be needed. It wasn't a vote. The more I did this, the more I learned that General Powell's point of trusting your gut was right. You get as much information as you can, consult with trusted advisers, and then make a call. Sometimes you have all the time necessary to get all the information; for example, when you do a formal bid process and receive quotations and references and can do interviews. But those are a luxury. The truest mettle of a leader is determined when the situation requires a decision without the luxury of time.

Takeaway: Seek input and guidance, but regarding major decisions, remember that as the leader, you have to make the final call.

- Think of times when consensus would be appropriate in your role.

- Also think of times when you have to make the decision. How can you ensure commitment for your decision?

- Have you had to make a decision based on a gut feeling? Did it work out well? If not, what do you believe you could have done to make a better decision?

LESSON 42

REMEMBER THE POWER OF VISUALIZATION

The key to effective visualization is to create the most detailed, clear and vivid a picture to focus on as possible. The more vivid the visualization, the more likely, and quickly, you are to begin attracting the things that help you achieve what you want to get done. (Georges St-Pierre)

Professional golfers stand behind their ball and visualize their shot. They see the path, a draw or fade, where they want it to land, the type of bounce, the spin of the ball, and where it will end. It's a proven method to see what they are trying to accomplish. Basketball players visualize free throws arching up and into the basket.

At the same time, coaches have learned that showing their players how to accomplish a task is much more effective than telling them how to accomplish it. Demonstrating a blocking technique is more powerful than describing the technique. For sales professionals, the old adage, "Seeing is believing," is a truism. They want to demonstrate product rather than describe product.

This is also true in the workplace. Mock-ups, prototypes, wire frames, and even PowerPoint presentations help communicate an idea and close a deal. Whenever you have the chance to convert an idea into a visual, take advantage of it. It can be a rough sketch or a sophisticated delivery medium.

The most recent visualization capabilities are 3D rendering and data visualization. Both are extremely powerful techniques that help in making decisions. Helping decision makers see the possibilities in a 3D rendering gives comfort and believability to major building and engineering events. Data visualization helps decision makers see relationships and interdependencies. In both cases, converting possibilities and/or abstract relations into visuals makes it tangible. Visualization works.

EXAMPLE

As an adult, I discovered the importance of learning styles. Throughout school and university, pure lecture classes were more difficult for me than visual or tactile classes (such as labs). One of my children shared my learning style. When given verbal instructions, we both would try to visualize those instructions. If we could write them down, there was a high chance of retention. If we could capture a vivid image, we could retain it.

At work, the pattern of visualization continued to surface: tools to prototype and demonstrate concepts, the need to sketch out concepts to minimize ambiguity, the power of 3D rendering and virtual reality, and now data visualization. Helping people see a possibility or concept is more powerful than just describing the concept. Combine the auditory with the visual, and it's even more powerful. Add an experiential element, and it is infinitely more impactful.

Visualization is a technique that pervades more than education and commerce. It is a tool humans use to see past the limits of their existence, to dream of better days and places, and to envision the future. The technique has been used for meditation to calm the nerves and practiced in childbirth to distract the body. Visualization has a place in everyone's personal and professional toolbox.

Takeaway: Try to always share ideas, concepts, or proposals in a visual manner. Use visualization to proactively envision an event or activity.

- When do you think using visualization would help you and your organization?
- How would you use this in your personal life?

LESSON 43

AVOID PUBLIC REPRIMANDS— DO IT BEHIND CLOSED DOORS

You don't lead by hitting people over the head—that's assault, not leadership. (General Dwight D. Eisenhower)

The adage, "Praise in public, criticize in private," goes back at least as far as 35 BC as attributed to Publilius Syrus. Management gurus over the centuries have advocated the process as a way to maintain the dignity of the person being reprimanded, and in current terms, help to ensure their continued engagement. Unfortunately, there are bosses who behave as bullies and do the reprimanding in public. In a culture that values respecting people, that behavior cannot be tolerated.

This does not mean there is never a time to publicly admonish a behavior. "What is done in public is corrected publicly" is another good rule to follow. If something is said or done inappropriately in public, a manager needs to speak up. If they do not publicly say something, people can get the idea that the behavior is acceptable or that the manager is hypocritical. When you have to do this, correct the action or statement, not the person. Then take the person aside in private, and speak to the specifics—and reprimand as necessary. By doing so, you make sure your team understands that you do not condone what happened, you are true to your values, and you correct the offending individual in a dignified fashion.

EXAMPLE

We had a senior executive who would berate people in large meetings for mistakes, errors, or even just for disagreeing with them. Given that many of the meetings were multi-level meetings or cross-divisional meetings, a large cross section of people witnessed the behavior. First, it was absolutely humiliating to the person being reprimanded. As a result, it created an atmosphere of fear and risk avoidance. Second, it formed a reputation for the executive that spread like wildfire. Third, others thought the behavior was acceptable, and they started to emulate that style. Ultimately, the behavior was denounced, and people were severely disciplined. In this case, the senior executive was coached, but others were not as fortunate. One vice president who emulated the behavior was removed from management.

There are times when managers have to call out errors or mistakes in meetings. When you do, do it without making it a personal attack. Pull the individuals who need counseling aside, and deliver reprimands privately. When doing that, again, work hard to associate the reprimand to the specific behavior or action and not at the person. By doing it behind closed doors, you give dignity to the individual and ensure privacy to the conversation.

Takeaway: Respected leaders do not publicly reprimand, criticize, or belittle their team members in public. Their public statements address the situation, not the individual.

- Have you witnessed a leader publicly reprimand someone? How did it make you or other witnesses feel? What should that leader have done instead?

- How do you want to be treated if you are ever in need of being reprimanded? How would you treat someone on your team?

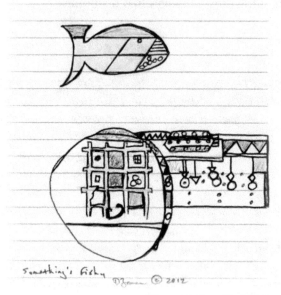

Figure 13: Something's Fishy

Figure 14: Quarters

LESSON 44

DO ONE-ON-ONES WITH YOUR STAFF

The day the soldiers stop bringing you their problems is the day you stopped leading them. They have either lost confidence that you can help them or concluded that you do not care. Either case is a failure of leadership. (General Colin Powell)

The practice of conducting one-on-one meetings with your direct reports seems to be an obvious management practice. But, amazingly, a lot of managers do not regularly conduct one-on-ones. Denying your staff the opportunity to have dedicated time with you is an injustice. You may view the one-on-one as your time to impart direction to your team member, but it is less your time and more their time. It is their opportunity to discuss what they are working on, their accomplishments, the issues they face, and the help they need. It is their opportunity to speak candidly and provide you with tough feedback.

To make these meetings as productive as possible, there are some best practices to follow:

- Commit to a repeating frequency. If you plan to do these every two weeks or once a month, schedule them for six or twelve months at a time. That indicates commitment.

- Ask your team member to prepare an agenda and send it to you one day in advance. This makes them invest in planning how to use the time and decreases the chance that the meeting will be an ad hoc, rambling discussion.

- Maintain a file or log for the one-on-one sessions so you can refer to prior meetings and follow up on discussion items.

- Allow your team member to add a section of candid *no hint zone* topics. If they do not, ask them if there are any things they think you need to know.

- If you have a list of topics to cover with the team member, save it for after they go through their list.

Some people believe that you should go to the team members' work space or a neutral place to conduct one-on-ones. This is intended to make the team member more comfortable. Personally, I think if it's more convenient for your schedule to do the one-on-one somewhere other than your office, it's fine. But having team members come to your office should not be intimidating. In fact, it's good for them to interact with others in your office space and to see the environment you choose to create.

For remote team members, it may be difficult to meet face-to-face frequently. Conduct the one-on-ones on video or conference calls. The important thing is to conduct the meetings.

If both of you agree there is no need to meet, cancel the session. But it must be mutual.

For some of your team members, this is sacred time. Help them make the most of it.

EXAMPLE

My boss was excellent about conducting one-on-ones. We may have had to reschedule because of valid conflicts, but we only canceled if both of us agreed. Generally, we followed the best practices. I created a template of sections: project updates, financial performance, items needing help, personnel matters, and no hint zone topics. Some of my peers did something similar but had a more strategic focus to their agenda. Others didn't do agendas at all and did the one-on-one in an impromptu fashion. How each of us approached it was insightful to our personality types and strengths.

Meanwhile, I tried to emulate the success of my one-on-ones with my boss with my team. We scheduled them months in advance and made every effort to honor the schedule. I typically had just a couple items to cover with each person, so the one-on-one was intended to be their time. If they prepared, it would be time well spent for them. If not, it gave me more time to not only cover my items, but also ask additional questions. It was in their best interest to control the agenda!

Takeaway: One-on-ones are a simple exercise with significant payback. Do not let the urgent get in the way of conducting these important sessions.

- Does you manager conduct frequent one-on-ones with you?
- Are there any of the techniques or practices listed above you should add to your one-on-ones with your boss or team members?

LESSON 45

RECOGNIZE MILESTONES SUCH AS BIRTHDAYS, WORK ANNIVERSARIES, AWARDS, PROMOTIONS

Appreciation can make a day—even change a life. Your willingness to put it into words is all that is necessary. (Margaret Cousins)

Team members love recognition. It can be for outstanding moments such as awards, personal achievements, promotions, and efforts going over and beyond, or being part of a successful team. The recognition can be for simpler, more regular events such as birthdays and anniversaries. Whatever the occasion, the simple act of recognition means a lot.

Empirical evidence proves that effective use of recognition drives employee engagement, reduces voluntary turnover, and improves overall morale. Employee engagement consultants Gallup, OGO Group, Cicero Group, and Globoforce have all researched and measured the impact of recognition. They recommend a combination of approaches that sometimes includes monetary rewards—but most times does not. Their findings suggest that employees overwhelmingly value recognition over monetary reward.

In their research, they also recommend making the recognition timely with respect to the event being recognized and the reward. Millennials in particular desire immediate recognition for their achievements, but that's not totally unique to their generation. No one really wants to get a work anniversary award eight months after the anniversary!

Suggested approaches to recognition are as follows:

- Peer-to-peer recognition awards
- Public recognition from senior management either in a meeting or through broad distributed email
- Organizational awards
- Personal notes, phone calls
- Monetary rewards

EXAMPLE

In my consulting days, we would reward team members with "Peak Performer" awards if they hit certain thresholds for performance. In a performance-based company, re-enforcing the goal of individual achievement and progression was important. In a people-based culture, we would give a combination of team-based awards, recognizing all the team members involved for their contribution to the success of a project, and a smaller number of individual awards. Each of these types of awards typically came with a plaque, an acrylic, or other form of display, and a small monetary award.

Meanwhile, on an individual level, I would send personal notes or letters to team members in my organization for certain events, achievements, or milestones. This recognition was a personal form of communication and did not come with monetary reward. Early at the start of a month, while my organization was of manageable size, I would send a short letter to each team member with a birthday or work anniversary in that month. By doing this month in and month out, I would see everyone's name, birth date, and years of service twice in a year. It helped me learn names and retain information about my team. I would sign every one of the letters, and for people I knew well, I would add a short note. I would also send handwritten notes, congratulating people on promotions, achievements, and other awards.

As the organization grew, it became harder and harder to keep up. Admittedly, when the organization exceeded one thousand people, I could no longer do the monthly birthday and work anniversary letters. But I continued with the handwritten notes.

Takeaway: Simple recognition of a milestone, award, or promotion is a positive re-enforcement of a leader's interest in and respect for his or her team.

- What type of recognition opportunities makes sense for your organization?

- What form should the recognition take (letters, notes, awards, etc.)?

- Research the importance of employee recognition and discover what the research suggests are the most valuable forms of and times for recognition.

CHAPTER FOUR:

CAREER LESSONS

FOUR: INTRODUCTION

No one other than you is responsible for your career and progression. You may have mentors and coaches, but they are not responsible for your life. They can help open doors and guide you, but you have to make the impression, choices, and decisions. You have to take the initiative and step up.

During my career, I tried to add new skills and reinvent as I progressed. Early in my consulting career, a wise mentor encouraged leveraging my education and training to add professional credentials. Thus, for my first two years of work, many evenings included two or three hours of studying for the Certified Public Accountant (CPA) exam. In college and graduate school, I had accumulated adequate credits to sit for the exam, but I had not taken all the relevant courses. So I had some gaps to fill in order to pass the exam. That required additional study. Passing the CPA exam wasn't a necessity for my consulting career path, but it demonstrated my ability to master a subject and to dedicate myself to a goal.

Next I leveraged the experience I was gathering in consulting and studied for and passed the American Production and Inventory Control Society (APICS) exam. This credential, Certified Production and Inventory Management Specialist (CPIM), was more relevant to my projects in the distribution and logistics industry and again demonstrated a willingness to dedicate myself to a goal. A few years later, I again certified my work-related skills by sitting for and passing the Certified Data Processor (CDP) exam. Fast-forward another few years, and I went through the process one more time to become a Certified Global Information Security Officer (GISO). This involved study of information security practices and technology, an exam, and publishing a white paper.

My strategy to reinvent and re-energize involved even more job rotations than credentials. I only worked for two companies in thirty-two years, but I changed responsibilities numerous times as I have already mentioned. Between studying to master a subject, working in different industries, and then working in different roles and functions within one company, I avoided becoming stale and bored. This strongly influences the first set of lessons in this chapter.

When people would come and ask for career advice, usually regarding progression opportunities, I would share the first set of lessons with them. First, if they were considering moving into management, we would explore the reasons behind their interest in becoming a manager. Second, we would discuss pushing yourself to grow and reinvent yourself every four or five years. Being curious and wanting to grow and learn are important attributes for everyone. Third, if immediate opportunity is not right in front of you, you might have to consider a side step or even a back step to move forward. Fourth, help your boss succeed by taking on more work or helping the boss with something very important to their career advancement. Fifth, look for the next big thing and carefully assess it. If it is promising, look for a related position with more responsibility and visibility. Last, when you feel a change in organization, position, or company is necessary, make sure you are moving toward a good situation and not just escaping a bad one. Sometimes the grass is not always greener. These are strategies I used in my career.

The next set of lessons focus on learning from situations in which you find yourself, managing yourself during your career, and making sure you present yourself in the best manner. For example, you can learn something from every boss you have, regardless of their style or whether you consider them good or bad. Next, you will have setbacks in your career and have to learn to deal with it. At other times, there will be risky opportunities, and you have to exercise good judgment as to when you should take the risks. Similarly, there may be times when you have to decide when to expend political capital and when it's better to not.

To complete this chapter, we finish with a set of lessons focusing on your personal development and behavior. Too often, people overlook little things that set role models and leaders apart from others. The first two are behaviors that leave a major impression: being punctual and managing yourself in social situations involving alcohol. I conclude with three important lessons regarding improving yourself to be successful in your career and be the leader you desire. The first of these three focuses on managing the dimensions of well-being: physical, mental, and spiritual. Nutrition, exercise, and diet are all critical compounds of physical well-being. Energy management, including sleep and rest, is vital to mental well-being. Spiritual well-being is important to wellness, and each of us must determine our own beliefs and path. Another dimension of well-being is personal hygiene and appearance. Rather than preach hygiene one-on-one, I will just say that leaders should set an example and take pride in their appearance. To quote the great sage Charlie Feld, "You gotta look good on a horse."

The personal development section concludes with two lessons regarding self-improvement: reading and public speaking. Leaders recognize their weaknesses and specifically work to improve. They always seek ways to learn, whether from their mistakes or the successes of others. They read and study to improve themselves. The final lesson is one that everyone can benefit from, regardless of their role and ambitions: develop or improve your public speaking capabilities. You don't have to be a great orator to lead, but it sure helps if you have the confidence to deliver a message.

LESSON 46

SO YOU WANT TO BECOME A MANAGER

You must know every single one of your [team] . . . you must be their leader, their father [or mother], their mentor, even if you're half their age. You must understand their problems. You must keep them out of trouble; if they get in trouble, you must be the one who goes to their rescue. (General Dwight D. Eisenhower)

efore you rush into management, take a good hard look under the hood, and make sure management is for you. Many corporations offer a class entitled "Is Management for Me" or something similar. The time spent is well worth it.

Management is a major change in career paths, and not everyone enjoys the role. A good "Is Management for Me" class will highlight the difference in work (contributor to manager), the personnel related challenges (performance reviews, motivating people, dealing with issues, etc.), the legal and bureaucratic nature of the work, and the role of supporting executive and senior management's strategies and policies. What the class may not cover is the human element of becoming a manager: taking on the responsibility to give every one of your team members opportunities to succeed, grow, and provide for themselves and their families. Every manager has the responsibility to care for his or her team, but not everyone who considers management has the disposition to do so.

EXAMPLE

When people would ask about moving into management, we would discuss their motivation for management. We had dual career paths for professionals and managers, so if the motivation was upward mobility, management wasn't the only path. If the motive was leadership based, we would discuss leadership roles both inside and outside of management. Then I would encourage them to speak to different managers they admired and ask about the demands of management—about the temperament to be responsible for others. I would share my perspective that, as a manager, they take on the responsibilities for their team members' careers and livelihoods.

Takeaway: Management is different from leadership. As we have previously discussed, people can lead without being a manager. Make sure the motivation to enter management is for the right reasons.

- If someone came to you and expressed interest in management, how would you counsel him or her?

- Have you seen anyone who entered into management and then regretted the decision? How could they have figured this out before making the decision?

LESSON 47

PUSH YOURSELF TO REINVENT & RE-ENERGIZE

We can't become what we need to be by remaining what we are. (Oprah Winfrey)

O ne piece of advice that I often share with folks is to try to change roles/groups/areas every four to six years. When I first began sharing this advice, it was during a period of growth and expansion for the company. The point of the advice was to expand skills, experiences, and perspective along with the company. Also, I felt that people could get pigeonholed or too comfortable in the same role after five or more years. So the intent of my advice was to re-energize yourself with a new challenge every five or so years, and in doing so, you would build a deeper understanding of the company. That in turn would make you more valuable.

Then technology accelerated at a pace that was astounding. My advice was still to rotate or change roles every five years, but the rationale now changed to "reinvent yourself to stay relevant." We move from one paradigm to the next quickly, and the people who could adapt would succeed. If anything, the suggestion might need to be changed to reflect an ever-accelerating rate of change. You need to adapt to a new paradigm of technology or strategy every two to three years to stay relevant. To do that, you have to constantly stay current and be open-minded to the possibilities of change. Never before has the need to reinvent yourself been more important.

EXAMPLE

In the consulting world, you change clients and projects so frequently that you quickly develop the skills to adapt to change. In the corporate world, some companies value rotation and broad, holistic views. They typically offer opportunities to re-energize and change roles. But others are more traditional, valuing deep functional experience in a specific domain. I was fortunate to work in both consulting where adaption was a necessity and for a company that valued rotation and movement. If I wasn't asked to take on a different role every three or four years, I would actively seek one. Over the twenty-two years of my corporate career, I held eight different leadership positions, with the last one being the longest tenure of all—six years.

In addition, as I previously described, I invested time and energy to build credentials and new skills as part of my reinvention strategy. So I absolutely believed in the advice I gave others: reinvent and re-energize every few years.

Takeaway: Proactively reinvent and re-energize yourself to stay relevant in a rapidly changing world.

- What trends or changes are occurring inside your industry or discipline?
- How might you grow within your current position? Can you do this with or without support of your management?
- How might you reinvent yourself for other roles?

LESSON 48

SOMETIMES LATERAL MOVEMENT IS NECESSARY TO ADVANCE

Sometimes you have to step sideways to get on the right path. (Anonymous)

The shortest distance between two points may be a straight line, but geometric law doesn't rule life. The straight line may be the shortest distance but also a very difficult route. Direct frontal assaults can work but at a price. Sometimes to advance, lateral movement is necessary.

This is very true at points in a career. The path forward for advancement may be limited by a well-rooted set of incumbents. The path to advance often dictates a strategic maneuver in the form of a lateral transfer. When done wisely, a lateral transfer can position you in an expanding organization, demonstrate a willingness to take calculated risks, and expose you to an entirely new set of eyes and circumstances. And there are even times when a step backwards may position you for the future.

EXAMPLE

As I left the consulting world, I could see opportunity in a corporate role, but the opportunity for advancement on hire was unrealistic. Rather than get that big kicker people in consulting expect when they join the industry, I chose to move laterally. The move had benefits, most certainly, such as less travel and being a part of a team with a meaningful purpose other than profit. But, most importantly, it positioned me with a management team that would create opportunities and reward performance.

Two positions into the corporate world, I volunteered for a lateral to take on a very risky new assignment. Two more positions later, I again volunteered to take on a new assignment through a lateral. In each case, the lateral move positioned me in new growth areas, gave me exposure to new constituents, and served to make me a candidate for future advancement.

As people would ask for career advice, I would always include the lateral as an option. If they were unhappy in their assignment, uncomfortable with their boss, felt limited in opportunity, or just wanted to do something new, a lateral movement was something to consider.

Takeaway: Do not think that all career moves will be solely upward. There are times you need to consider lateral movement to position yourself for future opportunities.

- Have you seen others within your organization move through rotations or laterals to build skills, gain exposure, or seek new opportunities?
- Have any of them progressed upward after such a move?
- What type of move such as these might make sense for you?
- Would a rotation or move help any members of your team?

LESSON 49

HELP YOUR BOSS SUCCEED

Take action where you are. Don't be concerned with who gets the credit. Assume more responsibility. Look for opportunities to support your boss/ help your boss succeed.
(Jimmy Collins)

People who are not satisfied with just completing their own assignments but are willing to take on a bit more responsibility are a manager's friend. The ability to share a task or responsibility can free the manager to invest extra time in a vexing problem, a potential opportunity, or a task. This is part of helping your boss to succeed.

EXAMPLE

This was a strategy that came from my consulting years. The consulting practice was a pyramid structure, and as people at the top succeeded, the pyramid would grow, bringing more opportunity for all. If you could help the person above you on the ladder, that person could stretch and do more. The effect would ripple to the top and the pyramid would expand. Staff assuming project management responsibilities lets managers concentrate on client engagement, and that lets executive members concentrate less on client delivery and more on client strategy and relationships.

This principle can be applied to the corporate world as well. The end result might not be the same, meaning that the benefit is not necessarily growth and expansion of the organization (unless in a sales type function) but more of a demonstration of growth and readiness to proceed to the next level. The ability to play up a level and free the person above you to focus on additional matters can differentiate you. Establish yourself as a dependable, valued member of the team. Then ask your boss, "What can I take on to free you of some responsibilities so you have more time and can be more successful?"

> **Takeaway: Reaching up and helping your boss not only reflects well on you, but it also helps the entire organization succeed.**

- How might you take on more responsibility?
- What tasks could you help your boss complete?
- If someone on your staff approached you, what tasks could they take on to free you to concentrate on more value-added activities?

LESSON 50

SEEK THE HEAT

Challenges in life always need leaders and leaders seek challenges. (Wayne Goodall)

A s you consider career choices, one piece of advice shared to me was to try to always land positions where investments were being made. Crudely, this was "follow the money." It's a very logical strategy. Identify what's hot, what the next big thing is, or what area is growing. Opportunities will come. Of course, with the heat comes some pressure and risk. But the inverse can also be true. Moving to a position in a stable, less visible function means fewer opportunities. Pressure and risk are reduced.

If a position is highly visible and is being supported by the executive team, it may be a wise career move—even if it is a lateral movement rather than a promotion. Seeking the heat demonstrates your courage, willingness to accept risk, understanding of the corporate priorities, and confidence.

EXAMPLE

As I counseled our next generation of leaders, they would ask about chances for advancement. And I would tell them to look for what group is growing. Right then it might be in one organization, but focus would soon shift to another area. I would ask them

> *to consider how to position themselves for the opportunities in those next big things: do they have the right experiences? do they have the right skills? and should they try to transfer laterally into the organization, anticipating expansion and advancement opportunities? Occasionally, people would ask about positions in less visible roles. Pursuing those positions for the ambitious could be good if the position filled a gap in experience or skillset. It could be a perfect match for someone reaching a plateau in his or her career.*

Be honest with yourself as to your goals, and select the path carefully.

Takeaway: Having the confidence to volunteer, seek high profile roles or risky assignments, or join fast growing organizations can help differentiate you from your peers.

- What groups or functions within the organization are growing, expanding, and receiving significant investment?
- Are there high visibility roles that need to be filled?
- Would any of the opportunities make sense as a rotation or lateral move for your career growth?

LESSON 51

RUN TO SOMETHING NOT AWAY FROM SOMETHING

Remember, you want to run toward that next job, not run away from your current one. (Bob Porter)

Tere are times when you find yourself in what seems to be an unsustainable position. You dislike your work assignment, you have too much pressure, and your skills and contributions are undervalued. The fight or flight instincts take hold and tell you to flee. But this piece of advice is to make sure that when you run, you run towards something that will be beneficial for you in the long run. Put another way, the grass isn't always greener on the other side. So when you consider options, decide if you are settling for a different situation just to get away from the current one or if you really are moving toward an opportunity. Changing roles is a very positive growth activity, but it needs to be performed with the right consequences. Use it to grow, not to escape.

EXAMPLE

Not every role I had in my career was perfect; there were times I needed to change, but I always tried to make sure I was moving to grow and reap future opportunity as opposed to just moving to get away from a situation. In the consulting world, the travel and uncertainty of assignments made me look for other opportunities. But I didn't jump at the first three or four that came my way over those ten years. I waited for one where I could see the upside of opportunity. Even as I left the corporate world, I did so with the idea that we were moving forward to a new adventure with personal freedom and untapped opportunities. I certainly ran a few times in my career, but I always tried to run to something.

Takeaway: Make your career moves deliberate, planned actions that are positive experiences.

- Do you know someone who has left an organization or company (to get away) only to realize they made a mistake and want to return?

- Have you ever felt unsatisfied or underappreciated in a role and wanted a change? Were you running from or to something?

LESSON 52

LEARN FROM ALL YOUR BOSSES— EVEN THE BAD ONES

You learn far more from negative leadership than positive leadership. Because you learn how not to do it. (General Norman Schwarzkopf)

Not every boss you will ever have is going to be a great one. There are bad managers. At the same time, not all bosses you will ever have will be bad ones. There are good managers. Regardless, you can learn something from all your bosses.

First, the good ones. When you are fortunate to have someone you feel is a good manager and leader, take advantage to observe and learn. Take notes on what they say and do. If your relationship is one that you can pick their brains on management philosophies and practice, do so. These are golden moments to learn from their experiences and style.

Now, the bad ones. For whatever reason, you may feel that you have a bad manager. Truly, there are bad managers. Maybe your style and theirs conflict. No matter, it is a situation where you do not admire how they manage or lead. You can still learn from them. Even bad managers can do something right. Look for what that might be. Is there one thing they are good at and you can learn from? More commonly, recognize what not to do. By noting what they do wrong, you can learn to not make the same mistake yourself. Sometimes learning what not to do is the best lesson a bad manager can give you.

In the consulting world, you would move from one engagement to the next and have a new boss almost every time. Sometimes you would be working for a great leader. But other times, you might be assigned to someone not as good. Since it was a pure performance-based model, you always worked hard, but when assigned to someone you thought was a bad manager or leader, you had to work twice as hard. During those times, I shared my frustration with my mentor, and he advised me to look for the one thing the manager does well and make note of the things I do not want to do when I am in their shoes. It was great advice since we rotated frequently. I did work for some great leaders, and one was a partner who taught me about caring about my team. This partner was from across the country and most likely would never work with this mix of consultants again. Yet she took time to get to know each of us individually. She learned about our families, our background, and what our goals were. She learned what motivated each of us, even though we would work together only eight months. As a result, we trusted her and wanted to do well not only for ourselves but for her.

In the corporate world, I had a series of strong leaders that I worked for and with. Over time, I had the opportunity to observe a few of the best leaders in Corporate America in many different settings: small meetings, large employee briefings, board meetings, customer settings, and more. During that time, I observed and made notes. Many of the lessons I have shared in this book come from watching how they handled and conducted themselves.

EXAMPLE

Our CEO was an icon in the business world but even more revered within the company's workforce. Whenever he was at a location with employees, he would take the time to shake a hand, ask a question or two, and connect with the people. I had a chance to contrast that to another legendary CEO at a Fortune 500 Corporation who had exactly the opposite style. We were together at an event, and this CEO did not make time for his employees. He ignored them, though it was obvious they wanted to have that one moment of connection with their leader. I observed and learned from another CEO at a publicly traded company on the importance of treating everyone with respect. He rode the elevator with the team and always held the door to see if there was one more person to get on board. He made small talk with everyone on the elevator and wished him or her a great day. As you exited the elevator with this gentleman, you wanted to run through a wall for him.

Takeaway: Every boss you work for can teach you some valuable lesson. Look for their good and/or bad leadership traits, habits, and styles.

- Think of your last few bosses; what one or two traits did you admire?

- Did they have any traits you felt were things not to do?

- Are there any exceptional leaders in your life? What do they do that you might emulate?

LESSON 53

WHEN YOU HAVE A SETBACK OR LOSS, IT'S FINE TO GRIEVE, BUT YOU MUST MOVE ON

Look at life through the windshield, not the rear view mirror. (Byrd Baggett)

Ultimately, you will suffer a work-related disappointment that hurts your heart. It may be a project setback or failure. It could be someone you trust disappointing you. It could be failing to get a promotion that you felt was yours, or a boss you love working for is transferred. Whatever it is, the hurt is real and personal. The human response is to grieve. And grieving is a necessary step in the healing process. In the workplace, it is okay to grieve the setback, disappointment, or loss. But you have to remember as a leader, people are watching you. People can empathize with hurt, and the vulnerability makes you more accessible to them. However, they need a strong leader who can rally back and press ahead. So, to paraphrase a famous expression, "To grieve is human, to move on is divine." Grieve, feel the pain, but as a leader, you have to timebox the process and move on. Your team needs that.

An additional part of this lesson is not to let your ego get so intertwined with a project or position that you cannot move forward. In today's environment, jobs and organizations are changing rapidly. You have to have the emotional fortitude to flourish in a changing world. Colin Powell said, "Never let your ego get so close to your position that when your position goes, your ego goes with it." This is brilliant advice for the twenty-first-century leader.

EXAMPLE

I had an assignment that I absolutely loved. The work was challenging, the executive team I worked with was supportive, and my team was great. Then suddenly I was told I was needed elsewhere in the corporation. Just when I thought I had settled into the pinnacle role of my career, I was being uprooted, and effective a month from then, I would be in a new role. This was a blow that hurt me to the core. On one hand, it was a great compliment that I was needed so desperately. But, on the other, it uprooted me from where I thought I would be for years to come, working with people I admired, and making a difference. So I grieved for my current role. For the first time ever, I was not energized to jump into the new job and attack it with the curiosity and energy I had always thrown into new assignments. But I was given wise counsel by a coach: "Grieve your loss for ten days, and then move on. Your new organization will be watching your engagement, energy, and enthusiasm. They desire and need the strong leader you are in the current role."

Years later I experienced another heartbreaking loss when one of my VPs chose to move on to new opportunities. As I have written, I would never get in the way of someone doing something to better themselves, so I cheered for this person. But not only was this a person I admired, trusted, and truly counted as friend, his spouse also worked with me, and I had as much respect for her as well. It was a double personal loss for me, and I grieved. Heeding the advice of my coach, I allowed myself to grieve and played that grief out in assembling a photo book

> *for the VP and family to take with them. I also orchestrated a going away party. But then, with a heavy heart, I had to move on and engage with the replacement with as much enthusiasm and energy as I could muster.*

Things like this happen to everyone in management; you have to be true to your heart but do what is necessary to move forward.

Takeaway: When unforeseen change or misfortune strikes, it is natural to grieve. But, as a leader, you must not allow yourself to grieve indefinitely. The team is looking to you for strength, and you must move ahead.

- Have you experienced this in life or at work?
- How did you or another find the strength to move ahead?
- Can you imagine scenarios at work where this might occur and how you would respond?

LESSON 54

TAKE CALCULATED RISKS

You have to run risks. . . . There is a precipice on either side of you—a precipice of caution and a precipice of over-daring. (Winston Churchill)

I n a survey of senior citizens, when asked one thing they would change in their lives, the number one response was "take more risks." They recognized that taking a risk is not a bad thing when it is done within a framework that assures the risk is not lethal or catastrophic and that the downside of the risk is well understood. This is true in personal life, in sports, in a career, and in leading an organization. Playing everything safe limits opportunities for a breakout success and can constrain creativity and innovation. Think about your investment accounts. Virtually every financial investment involves some degree of risk. At certain times, you may take more risk with your investments and at other times be more conservative. In both cases, you are taking calculated risks.

A wise leader weighs the risk/return for his or her organization just as they would for themselves. Being responsible for others heightens the importance of making good decisions but should not make a leader so cautious that they miss opportunities.

EXAMPLE

I never thought of myself as much of a risk taker. Personally, I was financially conservative, trying to avoid debt (and thus not leveraging myself) and living within my means. Professionally, I thought of myself as a plodder, not an innovator. But one day, my boss asked me to take on a new role that I perceived as needing a risk-taking, innovation-oriented leader. After expressing my concern about not fitting the role, my boss said, "Oh, you are indeed a risk taker," and that made me reflect on what I had done to give him that impression. Suddenly, I could think of a pattern of things that at the time I had assessed as good opportunities and the right things to do but apparently others saw them as more risky: advocating and implementing Apple Mac computers when the corporation was standardizing on Windows PCs; leading a very difficult and risky project that had material impact on the corporation; moving my family twice in twenty months for changes in positions with the company; stopping a product launch that involved a third of the company's revenue and redirecting the work for ease of use rather than new features; volunteering for new leadership positions where I had absolutely no experience. In each of those situations, I had consciously considered the risks and felt the rewards were greater. In one case, I still have the pro/con document that I had created to assess the opportunity. Only with hindsight did I realize that I was taking calculated risks.

Many times, career decisions are calculated risks. Many times, a change works well. But sometimes the risk materializes, and you take a setback.

EXAMPLE

During the dotcom boom, many corporate IT and marketing professionals jumped from lucrative career paths to follow the lure of instant glory and financial wealth. But few found the success, and many were out of a job when the dotcom bubble burst. Coming back to their previous role was difficult, given their positions had been filled and loyalty was being rewarded. In these examples, the reward was well understood, but the risk was underestimated. Many took a miscalculated risk.

EXAMPLE

From my personal experiences, I learned that it is important for a leader not to punish someone when a reasonable risk has been identified and accepted for good reasons. In one situation, we had to make a choice in how we allocated capital for equipment. We knew a new product line was growing rapidly and needed the limited capital, but at the same time, an older product line was riding on old equipment that also needed investment. We decided to take the risk on the old platform and invest in the new product. Unfortunately, the old equipment did break down, and that resulted in service failures. In our quarterly debrief, I reported the impact from the incident and explained the root cause, mentioning that we knew it was a risk but chose to take the risk. Our chief financial officer interrupted, and I girded myself for a lashing. But instead, he affirmed the decision to take a risk. He made the point that we cannot do everything and we have to make choices. In this case, we chose to take a calculated risk—one where the consequences were painful, but not catastrophic.

Takeaway: We have to take risks in life. Risk is not to always be avoided. Evaluate and assess when risk presents an opportunity.

- What is your risk-taking profile regarding your investments? Your career?

- Do you seek and accept opportunities with manageable risk? Or do you tend to play everything safe?

- Are there times you or someone else missed an opportunity because of being risk adverse?

LESSON 55

BE ON TIME, OR BETTER YET— BE EARLY

Players knew I used to arrive early for meetings and practices, and I expected everyone to be there and ready to go. Tardiness is the height of arrogance. In effect, you're saying "My time is more important than yours." Being on time is being considerate of others. (Coach Dean Smith)

I t is so easy to just do one more thing, look up one more fact, make one more call, or print out one more document before you leave for that appointment or meeting. Then you arrive five, ten, or twenty minutes late and make a terrible impression. Being on time reflects dependability. And when you are the central party in the appointment, being on time reflects a degree of respect for those with whom you are meeting. To keep people waiting is disrespectful of their time and a statement of arrogance that "I am more important than you."

Of course, there are times when urgent matters interfere, and you must run behind. In this case, try to send a message (text or email) and let someone know you have been delayed. When you arrive, always be gracious, apologizing for the inconvenience to everyone and thanking them for their patience. That helps alleviate the "I am more important than you" stigma. And remember, when you are planning your time to get to an appointment, factor in not just the travel time but also the time to get out the door, get to the car, go through security, find parking, go into the building, and go to the meeting room. Always know where you are going in advance (don't assume you can find Conference Room 3-B if you have never been there before), and if you drive, don't speed. You might save a minute or three racing through the streets, but if you have an accident or get a ticket, you'll be in more trouble than just being late.

EXAMPLE

Corporate America embraced the notion of off-site team building sessions. In our case, our leadership team was going to a retreat in the woods with nothing but basic accommodations, rope courses, and team challenges. To start the bonding experience, we were all to meet at 2:00 p.m. on a Sunday afternoon and board a twenty-seat van for the two-and-a-half-hour drive into the wilderness. Our colleagues from out of town were first on the bus. They had arrived earlier in the morning on the only flights that would get them to town in time to catch the bus. Others from in town started to arrive just before 2:00 p.m. But one colleague didn't show on time. Now this person was habitually late, so no one was surprised, and as 2:00 became 2:10 and then 2:15, everyone was chitchatting. One person explained how they got up at 5:00 a.m. to get to the airport for a 7:00 a.m. flight that morning. At about 2:20 p.m., people changed their expectations and started texting our lost troubadour, who responded, "on my way, be there in 10 minutes." Nearly twenty-five minutes later, the person arrived, and we set out. Of course, there was a story and excuse as to why traveling fifteen miles from home to the van was fraught with peril. Regardless of the believability of the story, the inconsiderate behavior—given that people could travel 600 and 1,200 miles and arrive on time—made bonding a most difficult task.

Early in my career and marriage, this was perhaps my greatest fault. I frequently tried to do one more thing, underestimated travel time, or just plain put my schedule and activities ahead of others. Truthfully, this was problematic enough that my wife insisted that we seek counseling. My disregard and disrespect for her time and the children's was horrible. At about the same time, I was fortunate to hire a great administrative assistant. Between a partner at home and a partner at work, I broke the habit of running late. At work, my assistant would text me fifteen or thirty minutes before the next appointment to remind me when I needed to be out the door. We actually tracked my percentage of on-time arrivals for a few months to help engrain the behavior.

Takeaway: People demonstrate courtesy and respect in a number of different ways. One is being punctual. Punctuality is one reflection of your character, which demonstrates how you treat people.

- Do you frequently run late to appointments or meetings? Do you know someone who struggles with punctuality?

- What actions can you take to improve your timeliness or those of a colleague?

Figure 15: Retirement Lunch

LESSON 56

NO ONE WANTS TO SEE A SLOPPY DRUNK

If you hoot with the owls at night, it's hard to soar with the eagles at dawn.
(Coach Morgan Wooten)

There is a camp that believes you can ride hard and wild as long as you can "answer the bell" in the morning. Party on, Garth. Then there is the camp that believes moderation is the better part of valor. In both cases, no one wants to see someone at a company or professional event get out of hand and sloppy. It's too easy to make the wrong impression, say something inappropriate, disclose confidential information, make unwanted or aggressive advances, or worse yet, drive while intoxicated, thus risking injuries and damages. The image and reputation that it leaves can follow you for years.

EXAMPLE

Our consulting firm was composed of a workforce that hired straight off the college campus. With an "up or out" philosophy, the vast majority of the team was well under thirty years of age. Training events and company outings could become rather raucous.

It seemed as though the only rules were "don't do anything illegal" and "show up on time the next day." So partying went well into the early hours. Occasionally, someone would get out of control and make a terrible mistake—causing a scene, trashing a room, or doing something illegal. They would be terminated. Mostly though, there were a lot of bleary-eyed youngsters in the morning.

Years later in my corporate life, I observed a much older workforce in out of town situations and company events. The percent of people partying long and hard was much lower, but those who did, did it with the same vigor of their youth. Amazingly, a similar result would occur. I still have the image in my mind of a drunken colleague with a straw stuck up each of her nostrils. Sure enough, someone would get out of control and make a career-ending mistake in a drunken stupor. Others would rally in the morning to "answer the bell" with a terrible hangover. A few might be able to "answer the bell" only to later slip away to sleep it off. The behavior was unacceptable.

If you do imbibe, ask a partner or friend to be a *power partner* and help you manage yourself. Empower them to cut you off and get you a ride or some other way home. Better yet, don't allow yourself to get so sloppy that you need help, make a terrible mistake, or cannot fully function the next day.

How can you handle company social events such as cocktail parties and long dinners with lots of alcohol flowing? Here are a few suggestions:

- Order a vanity cocktail, which serves as a prop.

- Order something you don't like and will only sip.

- One sales executive shared her strategy of having an initial cocktail and telling the waiter or bartender that for the foreseeable future to bring her a virgin version of that cocktail. With that strategy she could drink her compadres under the table!

- Or, just start out with a non-alcoholic drink and stick with it.

Most importantly, use self-control. Set a limit of two drinks or maybe two to three glasses of wine over a long evening, and stick to it!

> **Takeaway: Rarely does anyone look back on a career and say "boy, I wish I had drunk more at those business dinners and outings" or "boy, I wish I acted like a fool more often!" If anyone has remorse, it usually works the other way.**

- How do you manage yourself at business events? Do you have a mechanism or partner to help you moderate?

- Have you seen people lose control in a business setting? Were there any consequences?

- If one of your team members did this, how would you handle the situation?

LESSON 57

REMEMBER THAT SOMETIMES YOU CAN BE RIGHT—DEAD RIGHT

You can be right—DEAD right. (Claud Brown, Sr., Aka Han-Pa)

There are times when there is no question you have the right way and may proceed. However, it's a good practice to look and verify that the path is clear. This is because, as Ginny's grandfather, Han-Pa, would remind us, "You can be right—DEAD right." You proceed ahead without checking the traffic, and *BAM*! You are t-boned by someone who recklessly charges through the intersection. You may have been in the right, but the consequences are nevertheless horrific.

This analogy can be applied to many facets of life, both at home and at work. There are times in relationships where you can be right, but the consequence may not be worth it. Another expression we heard a lot at our home was, "Sometimes you have to choose: you can be right, or you can be happy."

While both colloquialisms make the point that being right can be dangerous, the intent is not to suggest that being wrong is a better course. Rather, they teach us not to assume, not to be cocky, and when our righteousness does offend, to be sensitive to the people offended.

At work, there are times when you may be right, but the cost of making that point might be painful. Is it a critical matter where being right makes a difference? Exert your political capital. But sometimes the situation is less consequential, and expending the capital to be proven right is not worth it. For example, embarrassing someone in a public forum (during a presentation or group email/text) to prove you are right may burn bridges or reflect worse on you than the person who made the mistake in the first place. For those who have raised children, you know to "pick your battles." This applies equally to work.

EXAMPLE

Truthfully, when driving, I may not be the most attentive to all the things happening on the road. Green light, go. Red light, stop. Stop sign, stop. Yield sign, look around. This is a major reason why, as a teenage driver, I was t-boned in an intersection. I had the green light, crossed into the intersection, and assumed all was good. Meanwhile, someone carelessly ran a red light and hit me while they were traveling at approximately forty miles per hour. This was the 1970s, and I was driving a boat of a Chrysler that had a lot of steel in the side doors. As a result, the brunt of the crash crumpled the front end of the other car and pushed the engine back towards the driver. My car absorbed the impact, spun a hundred and eighty degrees, popped a curb, and smacked into a telephone pole. Once I gained consciousness and crawled out of the far side of the car, I rushed to the other vehicle. The driver was pinned in, bleeding profusely, and in a state of shock. This was long before air bags. Police, fire engines, ambulances, and onlookers all descended, and I was escorted away to have my injuries tended. I never found out the full extent of the other driver's injuries.

What I did find out was that if I had slowed just a little, or he had accelerated a bit more, he would have collided directly on the driver's door rather than just behind the driver's door. It was that small differential in speed that determined if I was severely hurt or not. Years later, when I was driving Han-Pa somewhere and he reminded me as we approached an intersection that "you can be right—DEAD right," I realized how true it was. Even though I had the right away, I could have avoided the collision that night. Just looking and not assuming would have eliminated the possibility of being "DEAD right."

EXAMPLE

There were times at work when this certainly applied. In one case, our department was responsible for forwarding a monthly data file to our customers' systems. We were the delivery highway for the data. In that role, we could have been parochial and closed our eyes to the content of the file because that was the responsibility of the five or six groups that participated in a "Rube Goldberg" process to produce the file. Each department in the process added or manipulated the data in the file according to their business rules. They made assumptions about the rules always being applicable, regardless of what the group before them did to the data. But if and when that file contained incorrect or corrupted data, our customers would be severely impacted. We designed a verification process to test the data, but this required the other groups to participate. They refused, arguing they were responsible for the content of the file and our validation process was unnecessary and a waste of resources.

They were right in that the file was their responsibility. But they were DEAD right when they passed along a truncated file (that we could not validate without their assistance), which corrupted a large number of customer systems. The yellow traffic light we flashed before them was ignored, and they entered the intersection without looking one too many times. The sound of that corrupted file loading into customers' systems was metaphorically the equivalent to the sound of my car being t-boned. If they had not made assumptions and verified the final file, the incident could have been avoided. It took nearly a week and three hundred dedicated personnel to roll back that file and re-enable the affected customers. Needless to say, the verification process was eventually adopted.

Takeaway: Sometimes it doesn't help to always be right. There are times when you need to give ground and let someone else have the right of way.

- Can you recall a situation at home or in your personal life where you were better served by not insisting on being right?
- Are there ever situations at work when this lesson applies?

LESSON 58

TAKE CARE OF YOURSELF— EXERCISE, EAT WELL, AND MANAGE YOUR ENERGY

Lack of activity destroys the good condition of every human being, while movement and methodical physical exercise save it and preserve it. (Plato)

A career spans a lifetime, starting with high energy and expectations and progressing into leadership and responsibilities. During this journey, the natural aging process and the challenges of life and work place demands on your mind and body. To excel and be the leader you desire, you have to take care of yourself. You owe it to yourself, your loved ones, and the people you serve.

Let's begin with exercise. You have been told a hundred times to work an exercise routine into your weekly plans. Intellectually you get it; the benefits of regular exercise are phenomenal. Exercise works wonders for physical and mental health and gives us the stamina to perform in the many roles we play during a day: spouse, partner, leader, follower, volunteer, child, friend, mentor, etc.

So what stops leaders from regular exercise? The primary obstacle is an individual's perception that they are so busy they don't have time to exercise. It is one more thing to fit into an already hectic day. Reality check: even the busiest executive can find time for a workout. A secondary obstacle is that some people simply do not like to exercise. Reality check two: we all have to do things we don't enjoy at some point. With exercise, there are so many different ways to workout; those who dislike the notion might find a style that appeals to them and can be tolerable if not actually fun.

In both cases, the answer is personal discipline. In their book *Younger Next Year*, authors Chris Crowley and Dr. Henry Lodge write extensively of the importance of exercise and urge people to think of exercise with the same discipline that they think about work.[22] You have the discipline to show up at work. You can do the same for exercising. Consult with your doctor before starting an exercise regiment, and then read the short chapters on exercise in *Younger Next Year*. You can then develop a winning plan.

Similarly, we intellectually understand the importance of a healthy diet, but most of us fail to consistently follow the practice of eating well. It is too easy to let the pressures of the day dictate your eating habits: skip meals, then eat junk; rush and eat fast food; binge at an evening meal; consume too much alcohol. With some coaching, it isn't difficult to develop a plan to manage your diet. The principles of eating well are pretty simple: eat light and often, eat a balanced diet, always eat breakfast, hydrate, manage portions, limit alcohol consumption, and minimize pre-processed foods.

Lastly, you need to manage your energy throughout the day. In their book *The Power of Full Engagement*, Jim Loehr and Tony Schwartz explain the importance of managing your personal energy to be healthy and stay ready to meet the challenges of the moment—while thinking better and faster.[23] To perform at your full potential, you have to be rested and maintain a stable energy level through the day. Using their research and findings, peak performers in athletics and Corporate America manage their energy to help achieve their goals.

EXAMPLE

Growing up, it seemed that I always traveled in a cloud of smoke. My mother was a heavy chain smoker, and my dad loved his cigars. Neither exercised, and eventually, lifestyle caught up to each at age sixty-seven. In many regards, they were perfect role models, but for physical and mental health, they were not. Fast forward to my adulthood, and while I am not a smoker, I was not exercising other than an occasional softball or basketball league game. My preteenage daughter started to encourage, maybe even beg, me to exercise. I used the same excuses as most: I am too busy; I am in great shape; I will next year. Then peer pressure at work kicked in, and I started jogging.

Soon I discovered that I could compete against the clock, and I fell in love with the runner's high! I loved the energy burst you get from a good run. I saw the energy boost at work. I was more positive, and my self-esteem grew as I knocked off goals. In fact, I became so enamored with running races that I created my own t-shirt with a motivational slogan: "Don't Do Your Best, Do Better Than Your Best . . . Your Best Only Limits Your Potential."[24] With every race I was trying to do better and set another personal record (PR). Then I went a step further and organized my own 5K race, which introduced people to running and exercise.

As I ran longer distances, I learned the importance of managing energy. Obviously, the longer you run, the more energy your body consumes, and you cannot sustain the effort indefinitely. Continue without proper refueling and you bonk—or hit the wall. You need to add fuel to maintain your energy. For many amateur runners, refueling every forty-five minutes to an hour is a necessity. The same is true for professional golfers. You might have seen golfers such as Tiger Woods or Jordan Spieth eating a sandwich, apple, or banana in the middle of their round. To maintain their energy, they have been taught to eat snacks in order to avoid spikes and valleys of energy during competition.

Similarly, if you are a corporate athlete, you probably need to add fuel to your engine every couple of hours. A small snack of peanuts, trail mix, or an energy bar would do the trick. This strategy is not a replacement for meals. Eat breakfast, a snack, eat lunch, a snack, and then have dinner. Moderation in meals and small healthy snacks will keep you primed for your work.

Takeaway: Invest in your well-being as you would in your career skills.

- Do you exercise three to six times a week? If not, what stops you? How can you make a change in your life to build in exercise?

- Do you begin your day with some form of breakfast? Do you eat during the day? Is hydration a priority?

- Are you setting a good dietary example for those around you: children, spouse, family, and coworkers?

- Research the glycemic index, speak with a nutritionist, and plan your eating habits to fit your lifestyle and day. What snacks might you keep at your desk for a midmorning or midafternoon energy boost?

- Do you get adequate sleep each night? Or do you mistakenly believe that you can catch up on sleep over the weekend?

- Research strategies for managing energy and sleep on business trips across multiple time zones.

Figure 16: Better Than Your Best T-shirt

LESSON 59

READ LEADERSHIP BOOKS & STUDY LEADERSHIP

Not all readers are leaders, but all leaders are readers. (Harry S. Truman)

L eaders read. They read voraciously. They read to continue to learn. They read to hone their skills. They read to understand trends and opportunities. They read for inspiration.

Read biographies of great leaders. Read about history. Read about current events. Read about business and leadership strategies. Read fiction. Read.

EXAMPLE

If you looked down my bookshelf or my eBook collection, you would find a lot of non-fiction. There is fiction in the collection, but the vast majority is non-fiction. My top reads in each category are as follows:

» *Biographies:* Alexander the Great; Benjamin Franklin; Colin Powell; Condoleezza Rice; Dean Smith; Dwight D. Eisenhower; Franklin D. Roosevelt; George Marshall; George Washington;

Horatio Nelson; Jackie Robinson; John Glenn; Mahatma Gandhi; Nelson Mandela; Teddy Roosevelt; Thomas Jefferson; Winston Churchill

» *Historical Non-Fiction:* Doris Kearns Goodwin's *Team of Rivals: The Political Genius of Abraham Lincoln*; Stephen Ambrose's *Nothing Like it in the World: The Men Who Built the Transcontinental Railroad*; David McCullough's epics: *The Great Bridge: The Epic Story of the Building of the Brooklyn Bridge* and *The Path Between the Seas: The Creation of the Panama Canal, 1870–1914*; Mark Kurlansky's *Salt*; Lauren Hillenbrand's *Unbroken: A World War II Story of Survival, Resilience, and Redemption*; Jared Diamond's *Guns, Germs and Steel*; Sun Tzu's *The Art of War*; Rebecca Skloot's *The Immortal Life of Henrietta Lacks*; Scott Snook's *Friendly Fire: The Accidental Shootdown of U.S. Black Hawks over Northern Iraq*

» *Business & Leadership Strategies:* Charlie Feld's *Blind Spot* and *The Calloway Way*; Gary Gore's *Navigating Change*; Malcolm Gladwell's *Outliers* and *Blink*; Geoffrey Moore's *Crossing the Chasm* and *Escape Velocity*; Henry Nouwen's *In the Name of Jesus* and *Life of the Beloved*; Sydney Finkelstein's *Superbosses*; Stephen Covey's *Seven Habits of Highly Effective People*; Jim Collins's *Good to Great*; Tom Peters's *In Search of Excellence*

» *Sports Leadership:* Mike Krzyzewski's books, especially *Leading with the Heart* and *Five Point Play*; Daniel James Brown's *The Boys in the Boat: Nine Americans and Their Epic Quest for Gold at the 1936 Berlin Olympics*; Bill Walsh's *The Score Takes Care of Itself*; John Wooden's *Leadership Game Plan for Success* and *They Call Me Coach*; Sam Walker's *The Captain Class*

» *Journals and Newspapers: Harvard Business Review* and *Wall Street Journal.*

Takeaway: Find the genre that you enjoy, and read.

- Do you read current events? Newspapers and journals? What do the leaders in your organization read?

- Are there times when you can routinely read? Before bedtime? On planes?

- Do you prefer a hard copy book or is an e-reader comfortable for you?

- Have you tried audio books? Could you listen while working out, commuting, or traveling?

LESSON 60

TAKE A PUBLIC SPEAKING AND/OR PUBLIC RELATIONS CLASS

You don't have to be a great speaker, but it sure helps if you have the confidence to stand in front of a group and effectively deliver a message. (David Zanca)

O ne of the most valuable skills that a leader can possess is the ability to speak confidently in front of groups. The ability to relate to an audience and communicate your message is important. Of course, not all great leaders are gifted orators. Moses is a prime example. More recently, Lyndon B. Johnson (LBJ) got the Civil Rights Act, and the Great Society passed not through oratory but his honed leadership skills. But most of us don't have the same gifts and connections that Moses and LBJ had. We need to be as good as we can be in conveying our thoughts.

A public speaking class is the perfect place to hone your skills. One path is to read or take a Dale Carnegie class. Dale Carnegie helps allay the fears and self-consciousness that stops people from standing up and speaking. Some people use Toastmasters as a way to learn how to structure your comments, compose yourself, and speak in front of a group. Doing a public speaking class where the focus is on one-on-one feedback is very effective to improve your skills. In those sessions, you will be videotaped delivering a short speech. Next the coach will "go to the tape" and review it with you, pointing out what you did well and not so well. Then you go back in front of the camera. This is a humbling experience for those of us who do not like to see ourselves on video. The reward is worth it.

If you get a chance, go one step further and take a public relations class. The premise is that you will find yourself in situations where you are dealing with the media or employee groups asking tough questions. You are speaking on behalf of the organization and trying to manage a very specific message. In this training, you are taught to avoid using negative words and re-enforce positive points for your position. The training teaches you how to handle a very difficult question, address it, and transition back to your message. Once you have trained with a good public relations coach, watch various leaders and speakers, and you can immediately tell the techniques they are using or if they are not versed in handling difficult situations.

EXAMPLE

Many high school students participate in speech and debate where they practice speaking in front of their peers and a judge. The more gifted speakers typically win the competitions, while the others win at developing the confidence to stand alone, sometimes with little preparation, and deliver a message. I did this for three years in high school and loved the challenge of extemporaneous speaking. In this format, you selected a topic and had thirty minutes to prepare a five- to eight-minute speech. For me, the most difficult format was impromptu speaking where you had only thirty seconds to prepare yourself. My impromptu speeches were more improv comedy but unfortunately not very funny. Regardless, doing extemporaneous or impromptu speaking twenty times a year in competitions gives you the confidence to stand up in front of a group. That was my equivalent of Toastmasters.

EXAMPLE

Later in my career, we had the opportunity to work with one of the greats in media relations, Merrie Spaeth. Merrie had served as director of media relations in the Reagan administration and really understood the art of delivering a message. Working with Merrie's team at Spaeth Communications, Inc., was outstanding as they taught you both the big and little techniques of a calm, cool spokesperson. Not many of us in our corporate jobs deal with the media, as we have PR departments that specialize in that. However, the skills are absolutely applicable to dealing with any group that you stand before. You want to stay on point, use positive terms, take questions, and answer them effectively to show you are being transparent. Additionally, you always want to be calm and confident. I used this training perhaps more than any other training I ever received.

Takeaway: Public speaking is a valuable skill from which almost everyone can benefit.

- Are you comfortable speaking in front of a large group?
- Can you craft an engaging message and deliver it?
- Do you have the composure to answer questions from an audience?
- What classes, training, and opportunities are available to you to improve your speaking skills?

* View more lessons at *SpainwoodConsulting.com*.

NOTES

CHAPTER ONE

1. Sinek, Simon; *Leaders Eat Last: Why Some Teams Pull Together and Others Don't* (New York, NY: The Penguin Group, 2014).

2. Doug Guthrie and Sudhir Venkatesh, "Creative Leadership: Humility and Being Wrong" (*Forbes*, June 1, 2012).

3. Sara Ashley O'Brien, "Here's What's Wrong With Uber – According to Uber" (*CNN Money*, June 13, 2017).

4. FedEx Corporation, about.van.fedex.com, "Our People" (2017).

5. Reprinted with permission of the publisher. From *The Positive Organization: Breaking Free from Conventional Cultures, Constraints, and Beliefs*, copyright © 2015 by Robert E. Quinn, Berrett-Koehler Publishers, Inc. San Francisco, CA. All rights reserved. www.bkconnection.com.

6. See "I Am FedEx" videos at YouTube.com.

7. Listen to the author speak on connecting to a larger purpose at SpainwoodConsulting.com.

8. Aaron Lazare, *On Apology* (New York, NY: Oxford University Press, 2004).

9. Listen to the author speak about working in the field and doing customer visits at SpainwoodConsulting.com.

10. Reprinted with permission of *The Wall Street Journal*, Copyright © 2016 Dow Jones & Company, Inc. All Rights Reserved Worldwide. License number 4265401163306.

11. Jennifer Molina, "i4cp Study Finds Managers Who Cling to Good Talent Are Bad for Business" (Institute for Corporate Productivity, *Talent Mobility Matters*, April, 2016).

CHAPTER TWO

12. FedEx Corporation, Form 10-K, Securities and Exchange Commission filing, 2012, page 16.

13. Marianne Cooper, "The 3 Things That Make Organizations More Prone to Sexual Harassment," (*The Atlantic*, November 27, 2017).

14. Malcolm Gladwell, *Outliers: The Story of Success* (Boston: Little, Brown, 2008).

15. Geert Hofstede, *Culture's Consequences* (Thousand Oaks, CA: SAGE Publishing, 2001).

16. Sam Walker, *The Captain Class* (New York: Random House, 2017), 107.

17. See the video of FedEx Hub Air Traffic Control at YouTube.com.

CHAPTER THREE

18. Reproduced by permission of Kogan Page Ltd. From *Shakespeare on Management: Leadership Lessons for Today's Managers*, copyright © 1999 by Paul Corrigan, Kogan Page Ltd., London, UK. All rights reserved.

19. Larry Senn and Jim Hart, *Winning Teams—Winning Cultures* (Long Beach, CA: Senn-Delaney Leadership Consulting Group, 2010).

20. VitalSmarts, "Silence Fails" (2006).

21. Stephen Covey, *The Seven Habits of Highly Effective People* (New York, NY: Free Press, 1989).

CHAPTER FOUR

22. Chris Crowley and Henry Lodge, *Younger Next Year* (New York, NY: Workman Publishing, 2004).

23. Jim Loehr and Tony Schwartz, *The Power of Full Engagement* (New York, NY: Free Press, 2003.)

24. Shirts available at Zazzle.com.

ACKNOWLEDGEMENTS

I am indebted to so many for encouragement through the years to strive to be a better leader, servant, and person. That begins with the most natural leader I know, my wife Ginny, who has always believed in me and pushed me to be the best I could be. When we met, Ginny had a project on her hands. I was smart and ambitious but very unpolished. My leadership and servant talents were raw, to say the least. But, with her coaching and by watching her example as a mother, daughter, professional, leader, and volunteer, I learned.

And as I evolved, I encountered leaders who would teach me so much. I learned in person from people such as Fred Smith, Mike Glenn, Rob Carter, Charlie Feld, Michael Grebe, Kevin Humphries, Ken Spangler, Laurie Tucker, Dan Mullally, Julie Nelson, the Reverends Dave Hilliard, Tommy Edwards, and Wayne Curry, and countless others. I learned from leaders I never really met: Coach K, General Colin Powell, and others whom I could study. Then there are the leaders who worked with me to achieve some great accomplishments. I am forever grateful for the selflessness of leaders like Curtis Warhurst and Cathy Pugh, leaders who did not have a leadership title and did not seek one. And I have to say thanks to the hundreds of colleagues who encouraged me and supported me in my efforts.

When you begin the process of writing a book, it seems like a relatively straightforward task. Quickly you realize that it takes more than effort and dedication; it takes a team of friends and professionals who will give honest feedback and good guidance to bring the book to life. I am fortunate in that a number of friends and family have given me constructive feedback and encouragement. If I miss someone, forgive me, but I would like to thank my immediate family of Ginny, Nelie, and Ben, Peter and Elizabeth, and friends such as Dessia Nichols, the Bike Gang, Don Woodruff, Charlie Feld, Debbie Cain, Melanye Lunsford, Cathy Pugh, and many others.

After input and encouragement, the process turns to editing and production. Thanks go to Bart Dahmer and his team at

Innovo Publishing, LLC, Rachael Carrington (editor) and Yvonne Parks (cover designer) in particular, for working with me. It isn't as simple as I thought, but they made it as painless as possible!

Most importantly, I have to acknowledge the blessings in my life that have flowed from many directions, yet they come from a single source: loving parents, good health, a wonderful education, a great spouse, and outstanding opportunities are things I thank God for every day.

CPSIA information can be obtained
at www.ICGtesting.com
Printed in the USA
LVHW05*0420030518
575787LV00002B/5/P